THE ANCIENT
WELLS OF LLŶN

The Ancient Wells
of Llŷn

Roland Bond

The royalties from the sales of this book are donated to Ala Road Chapel, Pwllheli.

First published in 2017

© Text: Roland Bond

ISBN: 978-1-84524-267-1
Cover design: Eleri Owen

Published by Llygad Gwalch,
Ysgubor Plas, Llwyndyrys, Pwllheli, Gwynedd, Wales, LL53 6NG.
Tel: 01758 750432
e-mail: books@carreg-gwalch.com
www.carreg-gwalch.com

This book is dedicated to the memory of
Rena and Stewart Bond,
both of whom were born in Cornwall,
an area which has so much in common
with the Llŷn peninsula.

Contents

Acknowledgements

I would like to thank the following people who have assisted in the research and production of this book: all those who helped me to locate Llŷn wells and those landowners who willingly allowed me onto their property in order to inspect wells; Myrddin ap Dafydd for his help and support, and for his willingness to publish the results of this research; the staff of the Gwynedd Archives, Caernarfon for their assistance; Clare Smith for producing the photographs of wells which appear in this book and my son Jonathan for helping to sort the photographs and for putting them onto disc; finally, my wife, Enfys, for her unstinting support and for her forbearance in accompanying me on my many visits to look at wells.

Preface

It was as a young child that my attention was first drawn to ancient wells. My mother, who was born and brought up near the Cornish market town of Liskeard, used to recite a poem called 'The Well of Saint Keyne', a holy well which was situated close to her family's farm. As a girl she had memorised that poem and, on occasions, she was asked to recite it.

At about twelve years of age, while I was staying with relatives in Cornwall during the school holidays, I discovered Saint Keyne's Well. I remember being spell-bound by its quiet, secluded location amongst a mass of trees and ferns; I recollect being intrigued by the neat, small, square, granite building with gabled roof which housed the well. There and then, I made up my mind to find out as much as possible about that holy well and the saint whose name it bore.

Like Cornwall, Llŷn is particularly rich in historic wells and their associations with the Celtic saints. In days gone by those ancient natural springs were an integral part of the day to day existence and religious lives of the people who inhabited the peninsula. Many were considered to be imbued with great spirituality and extraordinary powers. Consequently a multitude of interesting practices and legends grew up around them.

This book, which is in two parts, seeks to shed some light upon these fascinating features of our landscape. Section I deals with the identification of and research into Llŷn wells; it briefly narrates the story of ancient wells in general from pre-Christian times to the present day but with particular reference to the wells of Llŷn; it details the different kinds of natural well that can be found in the peninsula; and it describes some of the many beliefs and practices that were once associated with them. Section II is in the form of an inventory which contains information about as many individual Llŷn wells as the author could identify by name.

PART 1. THE ANCIENT WELLS OF LLŶN IN THEIR HISTORICAL SETTING

An Introduction to Llŷn Wells

Llŷn and its peninsula stretches out into the Irish Sea with a north-east/south-west alignment. The Republic of Ireland, with which Llŷn has historical links, lies across the Irish Sea to the west, and on a clear day it is possible to glimpse the outline of the Wicklow Mountains from the northern coast of the peninsula.

The area covered by this study is that part of Gwynedd which extends from Ynys Enlli (*Bardsey Island*) at its south-western extremity to a line drawn between Porthmadog on the southern coast to Clynnog Fawr area on the northern side. Therefore it covers the ancient cantref of Llŷn and part of the old cantrefi of Eifionydd and Arfon.

The Ordnance Survey Explorer maps which cover this area (the 2.5 inches to 1 mile Explorer Maps Nos. 253 and 254) pinpoint hundreds of springs and wells. The majority are marked simply by the letters 'W' (well) and 'Spr' (spring), although 26 wells within the study area are identified by name.

Broadly speaking, there are two main types of well within the peninsula. Firstly, there are man-made wells, which consist of brick or stone-lined shafts, dug vertically into the ground to reach the water-bearing strata of rock. These man-made well shafts were often constructed on private property during the 19th and early 20th centuries to provide a convenient supply of domestic water for the householder and his family.

Secondly, and far more numerous in Llŷn, are springs – natural features of the landscape, which were in existence long before the dawn of recorded human history. Over the centuries many of those springs have been given names. These are the ancient, named, natural wells of Llŷn, and it is these wells, rather than the ones that have been sunk into the ground by human hand, that we shall be dealing with in this book.

It is important to remember that water is one of life's basic necessities, for without it living things cannot survive. Therefore, for thousands of years, the natural wells of the peninsula provided people with water for their daily needs. However, for many centuries, long before Christianity came to these islands, some of those springs were considered to be the dwelling places of gods, and they were used by the ancient peoples in their religious rituals. Later on, some of those pagan sacred wells became Christian holy wells. Some wells came to be regarded as agents of healing while others were used as a kind of oracle to predict a future outcome or to put a curse on an enemy. Around all of these special wells legends and folk stories were woven, some of which persisted in Llŷn into the 19th century.

These ancient named natural wells vary considerably, both in size and appearance. Some are simply hollows in the ground where water can be seen bubbling up in the corner of a field to form pools. Others pour forth from crevices in rock faces while occasionally a well is a *pistyll* (or waterfall) or even a small stream. Whilst many springs remain very much as they looked when nature created them, some were transformed by the addition of man-made stone basins to hold the water, as well as stone walkways, seats and steps.

Natural springs are not only prolific in the Llŷn Peninsula; they can be found great numbers throughout the Celtic fringe of these islands in places like Cornwall, western Wales, the west of Scotland and Ireland. When we consider these ancient water features several questions come to mind. When were they first used by human beings? How important were they in the lives of the people? Why are some of them considered to be 'holy wells'? When did those holy wells first have a religious significance? What caused so many of them to fall out of use and become neglected? And why, in the 21st century, is it important to be aware of these natural features and to conserve them?

The purpose of this book is to attempt to answer these questions, and hopefully to stimulate a little interest in this under-publicised and much-neglected aspect of our cultural heritage. Whilst there has been a great deal of research and much material published about many of our historic features, comparatively little attention has been paid to our ancient wells and the cult surrounding them. Most of the Llŷn guide books completely ignore them.

Without wishing to appear apologetic, it is important to recognise that the ancient wells of Llŷn are not easy to research, for much of their history is obscure. Therefore one has to be fairly cautious in writing about them. One can, of course, visit the wells to see what they look like and, over the years, the author has visited the vast majority of the examples featured in this book. However, some wells are difficult to locate because, even where their presence is marked on old maps, they seem to have disappeared. Certain ancient place names on old maps, names like Tyddyn Ffynnon, Ty'n y Ffynnon, Llwyn Ffynnon, Pant y Ffynnon and Bryn Ffynnon, suggest that a spring, or *ffynnon*, exists or once existed nearby.

Another serious drawback from a research perspective is the fact that there is very little early documentary evidence available about most wells, for much of the known narrative about them was written down comparatively recently, from the 18th century onwards.

Some wells are mentioned by poets and writers as well as by 18th and 19th century travellers to the area. Wells are sometimes referred to in Topographical Dictionaries and antiquarian books. Certain wells are marked on early maps, and little snippets of information about them may be tucked away in ancient documents like estate papers, newspapers and parish records. But very little documentary evidence predates the Reformation in the sixteenth century. Furthermore, there is a lack of archaeological evidence, for at the time of writing few Welsh wells have been excavated, and none in Llŷn have been investigated in this way. Where archaeology has taken place at well sites in other parts of Wales the digging has revealed no evidence dating from the Age of the Saints or earlier.

Many Llŷn wells are classified as holy wells and this is largely due to the fact that they were associated with early Celtic saints of the peninsula. It is significant that many of the Llŷn's wells are located close to ancient church sites and, in these instances, church and well nearly always carry the name of the same saint. Thus it is possible to establish a relationship between saint, church and well.

There is a scarcity of reliable documentary evidence about Celtic Wales in general and there is very little reliable information about the lives of those devout saints who established themselves in these parts in the 5th to 8th centuries. Many of the stories about the lives of those saints were written down by monks hundreds of years after the saints themselves had died, although a few details were recorded by contemporary writers. Nevertheless, most of the tales told about them must be regarded as legend rather than biography. Although those legends are an extremely interesting part of Welsh culture, the real lives of the saints remain fairly obscure.

One of the author's most important sources of information about Welsh holy wells has been Francis Jones's book *The Holy Wells of Wales* which will be referred to frequently during the course of this study. Another authority whom the author cites from time to time is James Rattue, whose book *The Living*

Stream endeavours to place British holy wells in their historical context. Locally, the excellent work carried out by the 'Llŷn Area of Outstanding Natural Beauty' team, as well as the writings of Myrddin Fardd and Sir John Rhys, have been extremely useful. The main sources of information about the lives of the saints are *The Lives of the Saints* by Baring-Gould and Fisher, the *Dictionary of Welsh Biography*, and *The Saints of Gwynedd* by Molly Miller.

Holy Wells before the Age of the Saints

In his book *The Holy Wells of Wales* Francis Jones states that the cult of the well 'had its origins in early religious belief and ritual.' Because many wells bear the names of early Christian saints such springs came to be looked upon as extremely sacred places. But it is generally accepted that the religious significance of the wells goes back much further than the 5th century. If that is so, we may ask, 'When did these natural springs first become important in the spiritual lives of the people who lived here?'

For a few moments let us look at the wider picture. Since the earliest times humans have attempted to make sense of the world in which they lived and their position within it. Things which they could not readily understand they attributed to a multitude of spirits or gods. They believed that powerful gods dwelt in the natural features around them and this resulted in a strong spiritual relationship with various aspects of the natural world. The sun and the moon, rocks, trees, mountains, thunder, lightning and the sky, as well as various water features (including natural springs), were believed to be the dwelling places of the gods who exercised a profound influence over human life. Therefore among the ancient peoples a water cult was originally bound up with the worship of water deities.

In ancient Egypt the god, Sobek, was considered to be the god of the Nile, while Nephthys was also worshipped as an Egyptian goddess of the rivers. The 2500 year-old stone statue of the ancient Greek water deity, Llissos, is to be found among the Elgin Marbles in the British Museum. In ancient Rome a nymphaeum was a monument dedicated to the water nymphs, especially those inhabiting natural springs, while the feast of

Fontinalia was a Roman celebration of sacred springs.

The archaeology carried out at Bath by Professor Barry Cunliffe has revealed that the Romans regarded the city's natural thermal springs as extremely important religious sites, for they built temples to their gods over them and used them as centres of healing. But Cunliffe also discovered that an earlier shrine at the Bath springs was built by the Celtic tribespeople who inhabited that part of England. They had dedicated the site to Sulis, a Celtic goddess of the springs. When the Romans came to Bath the Celtic name of Sulis was retained and linked to the Roman goddess Minerva. She became known as Sulis-Minerva. In fact, the Roman name for the town of Bath was *Aquae Sulis* – the waters of Sulis. The Romans threw huge numbers of coins and other silver objects into the Bath springs as offerings to Sulis-Minerva.

Therefore the veneration of springs, a strong belief in their healing properties and the practice of offering gifts to the water deities who they believed dwelt within them, was known to exist among the ancient peoples. In her article entitled 'The Religious Symbolism of Llyn Cerrig Bach and Other Early Sacred Water Sites' Dr Miranda Green emphasises that belief in the healing properties of water goes back a long way to Graeco-Roman and Romano-Celtic religion, as revealed through both literature and archaeology.

Going back even further in history, we know that wells and sacred water formed an important part of religious ritual in Old Testament times. The Book of Genesis tells us that the well by the side of the road to Shur was recognised as a holy well after Hagar had been visited by an angel there. The book of Exodus tells how Moses struck a rock with his staff at Massah-Meribah, causing water to to flow immediately from it to form a holy spring. The Second Book of Kings reminds us that the River Jordan was a sacred river to the Israelites. The

First Book of Kings mentions that the Kings of Israel were consecrated at the wells of En-rogel and Gihon, while pilgrimages were made to the wells at Beersheba and evil doers were punished at the Well of Judgement. In the New Testament the ancient well of Jacob at Sychar is mentioned, while the pool at Bethesda was believed to possess miraculous healing properties. The gospels record that Christ himself was baptised in the River Jordan by John the Baptist, and for centuries water has been used for the purpose of Christian baptism.

For thousands of years the concept of purification has been closely linked to the idea of sanctity. Even today, in many parts of the world, water is still considered to have special powers of purification – the traditional Jewish custom of purification by immersion in water known as the Mikveh or Mikvah; the ritual washing of Hindus in the sacred River Ganges; the Sikh tradition of bathing in the holy waters at the Golden Temple of Amritsar; the Muslim washing rituals known as *wudu* and 'ghusl'; the Islamic custom of partaking the holy waters at the desert well at Zam Zam in Saudi Arabia; the purification washing or 'misog' in Shintoism. Therefore we can be certain that the religious significance of water, and the cult surrounding it, extends a long way back into world history. Indeed the importance of water in religious belief and ritual transcends the boundaries of time, race and culture.

How far back, we may wonder, does the worship of 'water gods' go in Llŷn? We cannot be certain, but if we think about it carefully it is not difficult to accept that, for our early ancestors, the sight of a spring emerging mysteriously from deep underground, or bubbling up from a crack in a rock, must have seemed miraculous. Incidentally, the 'bubbling up' of the water in springs continued to be special in Wales as late as the 18th and 19th centuries, especially at certain healing wells like

Ffynnon Aelhaearn at Llanaelhaearn (see the details about Ffynnon Aelhaearn in Section II). We do not know exactly what form the well rituals of the ancient tribes took because there is no known record of them. Since a water cult was known to exist among the Celtic peoples we may assume that holy wells were important in Llŷn before the Christian saints arrived here.

Llŷn is particularly rich in evidence of Bronze and Iron Age settlement and activity. It is not the purpose of this book to describe and discuss in detail all that evidence, for it has been dealt with comprehensively in many other sources. Nevertheless, the evidence left behind in Llŷn by the ancient civilisations has a considerable bearing upon any discussion of holy wells. It is believed that, in the distant past, the ancient tribes had a close association with the water features which they found in the Llŷn landscape, and there was probably some sort of connection between those natural springs which they found when they arrived here and the man-made structures which they built and left behind.

1. A Bronze Age Water Cult

Following on from the Neolithic Period, a Bronze Age culture spread slowly across Europe, arriving in Britain in about 2500-2000 B.C. For years people tended to think of the Dark Age cultures as being primitive and barbaric. But more recent archaeological discoveries confirm that they were far from primitive. The Bronze Age settlers built and lived in houses, they farmed, they held religious beliefs, they traded widely, they made pottery, and they obtained copper and tin, the raw materials from which they made bronze.

The Bronze Age folk of Llŷn have left behind evidence of their settlement in the peninsula in the form of standing stones, burial cairns as well as archaeological remains such as Bronze Age pottery beakers, food vessels and various tools and implements such as bronze spearheads, blades and axeheads. Furthermore, evidence from across Britain and continental Europe suggests that water played an important part in the spiritual beliefs and practices of the Bronze Age folk.

We know that the ritual deposition of gifts to deities who inhabited natural water sources extends back to at least the Middle Bronze Age. Archaeological finds suggest that they carried out human sacrifice in honour of their water deities, depositing the bodies of their sacrificial victims into the water as sacred gifts. For example, a close examination of one early Bronze Age body, discovered in an Irish peat bog, indicated that he had been ritually sacrificed before being placed in the lake almost certainly as an offering to a water deity.

Much more plentiful in Europe are sites where quantities of Bronze Age metal objects have been recovered from rivers, lakes and springs. It is generally recognised that those artefacts had also been deposited as offerings to the water gods. For example, in 1980s, in the waters surrounding Flag Fen in Cambridgeshire, (a Bronze Age religious deposition site), Francis Pryor and his team found a host of objects, including weapons, jewellery and numerous small white pebbles which were not native to the area. They also discovered evidence of a wooden walkway which had once extended into the middle of the fen so that gifts could be deposited into the water more easily.

Items recovered at other sites across Europe are also believed to have been highly prized possessions which had been carefully deposited into water as offerings to a particular water god or goddess. Francis Jones points out that, in the Isle of Man, many churches were built on pre-Christian sites where Bronze Age objects have been dug up from the foundations and where invariably there was also 'a spring or gentle stream'. All this evidence suggests a continuity of use of such sites from the Bronze Age to the Christian era.

2. Wells and the Celtic Iron Age Tribes

Gradually the Bronze Age gave way to the Celtic Iron Age. The Romans regarded the Celts as barbarians but their weapons, jewellery, clothing, pottery and exquisite design remind us that they were far from uncivilised. They were skilled metalworkers, farmers, tradespeople as well as accomplished warriors. There is a wealth of archaeological and documentary evidence to indicate that they also worshipped spirits in the natural world, including water deities, for Roman sources confirm that, at this time, the Celtic peoples of north-western Europe revered water features as 'gateways' to their gods.

Texts and inscriptions dating from the Roman period suggest that the Iron Age Celts also performed ritualistic human and animal sacrifice, often on the banks of rivers and lakes, to appease or glorify their gods. The forensic examination of several well-preserved Iron Age bodies affords us firm archaeological evidence of ritual Iron Age human sacrifice. Three such examples are Lindow Man, found in a peat bog in Cheshire in 1984, and two examples from Ireland – Clonycavan Man (found in County Meath) and Old Croghan Man (discovered in County Offaly), the latter two examples both discovered in 2003 in peat bogs which had once been lakes. All three victims were probably of noble birth, and all appeared to have suffered deliberate and violent deaths.

Let us consider Lindow man for a moment. He had swallowed a substance containing mistletoe, possibly to sedate him, before he was violently put to death. Then his body appears to have been placed in the water at the edge of the lake probably to appease a water deity, perhaps after some kind of natural disaster such as a terrifying storm or a failed harvest. Numerous similar Iron Age 'bog bodies' have been discovered across northern Europe, most notably in Ireland and Denmark.

Many other archaeological 'finds' provide firm evidence that the Celts, like the earlier Bronze Age folk, also offered gifts made out of metal. In several European lakes large quantities of hand-crafted Iron Age metal objects have been recovered, as for example at La Tène on Lake Neuchâtel in Switzerland. Before being placed in the water many of those artefacts had been deliberately bent or broken, perhaps to indicate that all links with life on earth were being severed.

An important Celtic ritual deposition site in North Wales is Llyn Cerrig Bach (Anglesey), where a huge hoard of Iron Age ritual deposits was discovered during an extension to a runway at R.A.F. Valley during World War II. Approximately one hundred and fifty objects including weapons, slave chains, horse equipment, wagon tyres and other metal artefacts, were dug from the edge of a former lake. Today it is generally acknowledged that those artefacts, which are now in the National Museum of Wales, had been offered to the Celtic water deities, probably over a long period of time, as part of some sort of religious ritual. Llyn Fawr in mid-Glamorgan is another late Bronze Age/early Iron Age Welsh ritual deposition site at which metal objects have been found.

In addition to the archaeological evidence we also have important evidence from 5th to 7th century Christian documentary sources. The Ecclesiastical Council of Arles in 452, denounced those 'who offer vows to trees or wells or stones, as they would at altars.' A century later, in 567, the Council of Tours issued a decree that 'every priest industriously advance Christianity and extinguish heathenism, and forbid the worship of fountains.' A few years later in 574

Saint Martin of Braga wrote, 'To burn candles at stones and trees and springs... what is that but the worship of the devil.' Saint Gildas, a Brythonic monk and Latin scholar, also writing in the 6th century, attacked pagan beliefs in '*mountains, fountains, hills...*' The inclusion of the words 'fountains', 'wells' and 'springs' in those pronouncements is significant because it provides clear contemporary documentary evidence that wells and springs were being revered as holy places by the Celtic tribes of Europe at a time when the missionaries from Rome and the Celtic saints were seeking to spread their message.

James Rattue agrees that there was already 'an established native water-cult when the Romans invaded these islands' and that 'the Celts in Britain were wont to incorporate monuments of previous cultures within their own.' (Rattue *The Living Stream*, 1995) Therefore it would appear that the Celtic tribespeople had an affinity with, and a reverence for, not only the water deities who they believed dwelt in rivers, lakes and springs but also for the megaliths which were present within the landscape when they arrived.

Who were these folk who worshipped gods in springs and other natural features, who fashioned objects out of iron, and who colonised Llŷn? The Celts consisted of various tribes who spoke a Celtic language and who had a similar culture. We know that, following on from the Bronze Age, Llŷn was inhabited by scattered warring tribes of Goidel-speaking Celtic folk who had sailed across from Ireland. Known to the Romans as the Gangani – the Roman writer, Ptolemy, referred to Llŷn as 'the promontory of the Gangani' – they had migrated to Llŷn from that part of Ireland which we now know as Leinster. The old spelling 'Lleyn' comes from the same derivation as the Irish word 'Leinster'.

It was not only springs and larger bodies of water, such as lakes and rivers, that the Celts venerated, for it is known that they also had a special spiritual relationship with certain kinds of trees. Francis Jones and Val Shepherd have both pointed out that, in various parts of Wales, several kinds of tree are associated with wells. It is known that the hawthorn was one of the trees which had a special religious significance for certain Celtic tribes. With its white spring blossom it was considered to be not only a holy tree which protected against evil but also one that was sacred to the 'White Goddess' who regenerated the spring each year. Robert Graves, in his book *The White Goddess*, reminds us that it was predominantly the sacred hawthorn which grew over wells in the Goidelic areas of Britain. Before the arrival of Cunedda and his Brythonic-speaking tribe, Llŷn was a region where the tribespeople spoke a Goidelic language. Therefore it is believed that the Goidelic-speaking tribes of Llŷn revered the sacred hawthorn.

It is certainly true that hawthorn trees are mentioned frequently in writings about Llŷn wells. Written antiquarian accounts of practices carried out at many of the peninsula's wells during the Christian era involved casting thorns from a hawthorn tree into the water as offerings, or hanging pieces of rag or sheep's wool on the branches of an overhanging or nearby hawthorn tree. Furthermore, there used to be a commonly-held belief that to disturb or damage an old hawthorn tree at a well site would invite disastrous consequences. An ancient legend associated with Ffynnon Ddigwig (at Penarth near Clynnog Fawr) prophesied that devastating thunder and lightning would erupt if ever the nearby hawthorn tree was chopped down. And so we are led to the conclusion that there was a strong spiritual association for the Celts of Llŷn between wells and hawthorn trees.

When did the worship of these pagan gods cease to be commonplace in Llŷn? We cannot be certain, but it has to be assumed that worship of pagan deities was common in the peninsula until the majority of the local tribespeople had been converted to Christianity by the Celtic saints, although it is clear that certain pagan practices and superstitions continued in Llŷn long into the future.

Although Roman Christianity came to Wales early in the 4th century, following the 'partial conversion' of the Roman Emperor Constantine, it is clear that the inhabitants of Llŷn remained untouched by this new religion. While there is some evidence of early adherence to Roman Christianity in south-eastern Wales – a Roman vessel with a Chi-Ro Christian symbol was found at Caerwent, and it is recorded that, in the 4th century, two Christians, Aaron and Julius, were martyred in Caerleon – as far as Llŷn is concerned the Celtic Iron Age folk of the peninsula remained virtually isolated from the Roman way of life, and therefore from Roman Christianity.

Archaeological evidence associated with the Romans, or rather the absence of it, confirms that the Romans did not thoroughly colonise the mountainous area of northern Wales and Llŷn beyond it. They probably considered it militarily and economically unimportant. The nearest important Roman fort to Llŷn was near the coast at *Segontium* (Caernarfon) which was the Roman military and administrative centre for north-western Wales. A smaller auxiliary Roman fort was constructed on a flat-topped hill at Pen Llystyn, Dolbenmaen, almost certainly to command one of the chief natural routes across that part of Wales. Furthermore, a Roman bath house with hypocaust (warm air under-floor central heating) has been excavated at Tremadog. Although the Roman troops probably made the occasional foray into Llŷn, from either Pen Llystyn or Segontium, there is a glaring absence of Roman archaeology further down the peninsula itself.

This lack of Roman archaeological evidence within the peninsula suggests that the Celtic tribes who constructed their forts on Llŷn hill tops were, for the most part, left alone by the Romans to live their lives according to their own native culture. And therefore it is probable that the well-worship of the Celtic tribes continued undisturbed in the peninsula throughout the Roman occupation of these islands.

3. The Relationship between Llŷn Wells and the Structures Built by the Ancient Tribes

Francis Jones writes that 'well-worship was a feature of the religious life of the Ancients, being associated with gods, oracles, festivals, and with burials, megaliths and trees.' A close examination of the map of Llŷn reveals that many of the peninsula's ancient wells are located fairly close to Bronze Age and Iron Age sites, such as the standing stones at Glasfryn and Betws Fawr (Llanystumdwy); the burial cairns at places like Mynydd Carnguwch, Mynydd Rhiw and Garn Fadrun; the hill top forts at Tre'r Ceiri, Garn Boduan, Garn Fadrun, Pen y Gaer, Castell Odo, Castell Caeron, Conion, Wyddgrug and Garn Pentrych; and the hut groups at Llanaelhaern, Carnguwch, Penarth, Saethon and Rhiw.

Bearing all this in mind, and with the knowledge that the Bronze Age and Iron Age peoples who inhabited most of Europe worshipped water deities at special sites including natural wells, we may be led to the conclusion that some of the Llŷn wells must have been religious sites before the Christian saints arrived here, especially those springs which were fairly close to the places where the ancient tribes had settled and built their structures. Subsequently, as we shall see in the next section, there is considerable evidence to show that the Christian saints took over and continued to use certain pagan religious sites, including ancient holy wells. Futhermore, it was not only pagan holy wells that were utilised by the Christians.

We know that other pagan religious sites in Britain were also Christianized, as for example in the case of a Dorset pagan earth circle or henge, which became a Christian site and within the confines of which Knowlton Church was subsequently built.

Llŷn Wells and Early Christianity

We have seen how Roman Christianity had not come to Llŷn by the time the Roman legions left Wales during the first decade of the 5th century. Some time later, probably towards the end of the same century, the first Celtic Christian saints arrived in Llŷn, and it was those early saints who first brought the Christian message to this peninsula and its offshore islands. They journeyed extensively in a world where travel was difficult and dangerous. They sailed in small boats along the ancient, well-established sea trading routes, and they tramped on foot mile after mile over inhospitable terrain. Some even sailed into the Mediterranean to visit the Holy Land while a few seem to have ventured as far as India.

They were adventurous, determined, authoritative and knowledgable individuals. Many came from the high status class of the warrior prince and the tribal leader. They were frequently able to establish relationships with local Celtic rulers and this greatly assisted them in their missionary endeavours. It is possible, of course, to establish a link between the Celtic Christian missionaries and many of the peninsula's natural springs and settlements because their names are attached to so many of them.

1. The Missionary Work of the Celtic Christian Saints

Against all the odds, those Celtic missionary saints were responsible for undertaking perhaps the most difficult and most successful evangelising mission that Wales has ever seen. Over several centuries they converted to Christianity many of the pagan Celts. This must have been a dangerous time to be travelling in unfamiliar lands, preaching the Christian gospel. There are tales of Christian saints (like Saint Germanus) gathering armies together in order to attack and drive away hostile invaders, for in many ways they were 'men of their time'.

The missionary cause of the Llŷn saints must have been helped greatly by the presence in these parts of the warrior-leader, Cunedda, and his Brythonic-speaking people who, towards the end of the 4th century, had travelled from 'The Old North', beyond Hadrian's Wall, to settle the northern part of Wales. There was a long-standing cultural affinity between Wales and the southern part of Scotland. Cunedda and his tribe travelled southwards to establish themselves in northern Wales where they attempted to secure the area from further Irish invasions. During the 4th century, according to Gildas, the Irish were invading western Wales more frequently and in greater numbers, for he wrote that they appeared 'like dark swarms of worms which emerge from their holes in the heat of the noonday sun.' (Cited by Griffiths in *TCHS* Vol. 7 1946)

It is generally accepted that, before moving southwards, Cunedda had already come under Roman and Christian influence, for his sons had been given Christian names. There is a theory that Cunedda's grandfather had been given the task of defending the Roman Empire in southern Scotland against the hostile Picts. It has also been argued that Cunedda may have been given a military command by Imperial Rome, and that he had been despatched to northern Wales by the Romans, with orders to defend this part of the disintegrating Roman Empire against the invading Irish. The use of local native militia units by Imperial Rome in defence of the borders of their Empire was certainly not unusual.

Cunedda and his tribe seemed to be very successful in repelling further Irish invasions and so, in his new homeland, Cunedda was able to establish some stability and a semblance

Aberdaron – Ffynnon Saint

Aberdaron: Ffynnon Saint, well and cover

Abererch: Ffynnon Cawrdaf

Bryncroes: Ffynnon Fair

Clynnog Fawr: Ffynnon Beuno

Clynnog Fawr: Ffynnon Beuno, the interior

Llanaelhaearn: Ffynnon Aelhaearn

Llandudwen – Ffynnon Dudwen

36

Llanengan – Ffynnon Engan

Llangybi: Ffynnon Gybi, exterior

Llangybi: Ffynnon Gybi, exterior

Llangybi: Ffynnon Gybi, exterior

Llangybi: Ffynnon Gybi, steps to interior pool

Llangybi: Ffynnon Gybi, interior pool

Mynytho: Ffynnon Fyw, namestone

Mynytho: Ffynnon Fyw, overgrown

Mynytho: Ffynnon Sarff

Mynytho: Ffynnon Fyw,restoration work

Nefyn: Ffynnon Fair

Pwllheli: Ffynnon Felin Bach

Pwllheli: Ffynnon Felin Bach, the slate

Nefyn: Ffynnon Mynydd Nefyn

Pentrefelin: Ffynnon Ddunawd

Ynys Enlli (Bardsey): from Capel Mair above Ffynnon Fair

Ynys Enlli (Bardsey): believed to be Ffynnon Corn

Ynys Enlli (Bardsey): the gate on Ffynnon Corn

Ynys Enlli (Bardsey): the abbey ruins

Ynys Enlli (Bardsey): Ffynnon Dolysgwydd

47

Ynys Enlli (Bardsey): Ffynnon Waen Cristin

Ynys Enlli (Bardsey): Ffynnon Weirglodd Bach

of political unity. Under his leadership, and later under that of his descendents, there gradually emerged a new society in this part of Wales, where the early foundations of the kingdom of Gwynedd were firmly laid. Having established relationships with some of the local rulers, especially the descendants of Cunedda, many of the early saints were able to enjoy a measure of royal patronage.

When the first Christian saints came to the peninsula by sea, they brought with them, not only the Christian gospel, but also other influences, including the written language of the Romans, for Latin was the language of scholarship within the early Celtic Christian Church. That is why Latin inscriptions, carved on stones during the Age of the Saints, have been found in Llŷn, as for example at Plas Glyn y Weddw (Llanbedrog) and in Saint Hywyn's Church (Aberdaron). Other ancient inscribed stones can be seen in the churches and churchyards at Llannor, Llanaelhaearn, Llangwnnadl and Llangian. These stones were set up during the 5th, 6th and 7th centuries to mark the burial sites of significant local Christian figures.

Although Celtic Christianity and the Roman Church evolved from the same beginnings, there were significant differences between them. The Celtic Christians owed a great deal to the strict, ascetic, monastic tradition of the Desert Fathers (like Saint Anthony) who had settled in the Middle East, mainly in the desert areas of Egypt, to live out their lives in contemplation, devotion and self denial. There was no central leader among the Celtic Christians as there was in the Roman Church and, whilst a saint of the Church of Rome was someone who had been recognised as such by the church hierarchy, the Celtic term 'saint' referred to any person, man or woman, who had devoted his or her entire life to the service of God. There were also certain doctrinal differences between these two strands of Christianity.

The saints of Llŷn were greatly influenced by other Celtic areas, especially Brittany, Cornwall and Ireland. The first Celtic saints probably arrived in Llŷn from Brittany towards the end of the 5th century. According to *The Book of Llandaff* Saint Cadfan, who was probably of noble birth, established a monastery at Tywyn in about 516, before he came to Llŷn to found the community of monks on Ynys Enlli. However, there were almost certainly Celtic saints in Llŷn before the establishment of the religious community on Enlli. Therefore Llŷn was one of the cradles of Christianity in these islands.

Some of the first Celtic saints in Llŷn settled in remote locations to live as hermits, while others established small Christian communities. Over time, small settlements grew up around many of the places where the saints had settled. Today large numbers of Llŷn villages still remind us of their associations with Celtic saints like Aelhaearn, Pedrog, Edern, Ceidio, Iestyn, Tudwen, Cian, Engan, Gwynhoedl, Buan, Dwrdan, Merin, Maelrhys and Cybi. Those early Christian figures are commemorated today in local place names such as Llanaelhaearn, Llanbedrog, Edern, Ceidio, Llaniestyn, Llandudwen, Llangian, Llanengan, Llangwnnadl, Boduan, Bodwrdda, Bodferin, Llanfaelrhys and Llangybi.

Professor Bowen (*The Saints of Gwynedd*), states that, from the 5th to the 8th centuries, there evolved three distinct types of religious establishment at sites where the Celtic saints settled. Firstly there were mother churches, each a combination of monastery and college (usually referred to as a 'clas') where priests and lay monks lived together under the leadership of an abbot, worshipping and teaching. Secondly there were smaller religious settlements, containing a few huts and a small wooden church, situated within a circular or oval burial enclosure called a 'llan'. And thirdly there were individual cells where solitary hermits established themselves to live lives of devotion and self-denial. Examples of all three types of settlement are to be found in Llŷn to this day. Saint Beuno's monastery at Clynnog Fawr was a clas, as was the religious community at Aberdaron; there are numerous examples of 'llannau' throughout the peninsula, as evidenced by their names ('Llan plus the name of a local saint'); and it seems that Bodwrdda (*bod* meaning 'home' plus the name Dwrdan) and Boduan (*bod* plus Buan) were places where solitary hermits called Dwrdan and Buan established themselves.

When the name of a Celtic saint is attached to a llan it is usually, although not always, an indication of a site of great antiquity. Hilling writes, 'A large proportion of the churches that exist today in Wales – although rebuilt in later centuries – were originally founded in these early Christian times, and this may account for their often isolated positions in far valleys and on remote moorlands. The circular or oval boundary wall of the llan, in which many of them still stand, testify to their great antiquity.' (Hilling: *The Historic Architecture of Wales*)

It cannot have been by accident that many of those early llannau were established close to existing natural wells. Francis Jones has recorded nearly 200 examples of Welsh churches and well-chapels built at or near holy wells, including many in Llŷn. In such cases it was not only the 'llan' that took the name of the saint but also the nearby holy well.

2. The Christianization of Llŷn Pagan Wells

The conversion of the Llŷn Celtic tribes to Christianity must have been a long and arduous process. We know, from the statements issued by the Councils of the Roman Church in the 5th and 6th centuries, and from the writings of the saints Gildas and Martin of Braga, that the Christian missionaries were experiencing difficulties in overcoming the old pagan ways.

It is now accepted by most historians that certain natural springs revered by the pagans were taken over and Christianized by the incoming saints. One writer has written, 'Holy wells... are generally believed to have been places of pagan veneration which were dedicated and perhaps adopted as baptismal foci during the Christian Conversion.' (Rodwell 1980, cited by J. Rattue) Another wrote, 'The tradition of worship at wells was deeply embedded in the pagan mind. Christianity redirected these observances, and saints presided over the benefits attributed to the waters.' (Vince 1978, cited by J. Rattue) R. Geraint Jones confirms that 'the Christian pioneers were... skilful enough to use sites already regarded as holy as the bases for their own missionary activity.'

Therefore, we may conclude that the early saints set up their bases near to wells not simply to obtain water for their daily needs and for use during Christian ritual, but also as a way of appealing to the spiritual instincts of the pagan tribespeople who had traditionally carried out their own sacred rituals there. There is documentary evidence from early 7th century Christian sources, indicating that the missionaries from Rome were instructed by the Pope to take over and make use of pagan wells.

In 601 Pope Gregory issued instuctions that the pagan aspects of the old religion ('the idols') were to be abolished but the familiar places which the tribes revered ('the temples') were to be retained. He wrote to Saint Mellitus thus, 'We have come to the conclusion that the temples of the idols... should on no account be destroyed. The idols are to be destroyed, but the temples themselves should be aspersed with holy water, alters set up in them, and relics deposited there... In this way we hope that the people, seeing that their temples are not destroyed, may abandon their error.' This papal instruction leads us to the conclusion that the Christianization of pagan 'temples' like wells, certainly did occur, but we must be cautious, for we have no reason to believe that all pagan sacred wells were taken over and used in this way.

It is not surprising that the saints should have consecrated certain wells and made use of them in converting the local population, for they would surely have recognised the religious significance of water. Prior to arriving in Llŷn, men like Cadfan, Lleuddad, Beuno, Cybi, Pedrog and the other saints, would already have been aware of the numerous Biblical references to it. In fact the scriptures abound with references to 'wells and springs' 'living waters', 'healing waters', 'fountains', and 'streams'.

Therefore some of the old pagan wells continued to be used for Christian baptism, for the washing of sacred vessels and as a way of appealing to the instincts of the pagan Llŷn tribespeople. However, such places now had a very different meaning, for they had become important 'temples' in the evangelising work of the Christian saints.

And so, over several centuries, many of the old pagan gods were banished to be replaced by the Christian God. During this process certain of the ancient religious sites remained but with a new meaning – and that included some of the old pagan holy wells. In this way the saints were able to 'direct the faltering steps of doubting Britons on the road of Christian salvation,' as Francis Jones has put it.

But old traditions die hard and the eradication of pagan belief and practice among the population of Llŷn was far from complete by the time the Normans invaded southern England in 1066. Rattue points out that in England heathen practices such as the 'worship of wells, and necromancy (i.e. witchcraft), and worship of trees and worship of stones' were still being documented during 10th and 11th centuries. Myrddin Fardd informs us that the water from one well in Pistyll was still being used for the purposes of witchcraft in fairly modern times while, as late as the second half of the nineteenth century, certain wells continued to be used for superstitious practices like prophecy and for cursing enemies.

3. Dating Early Christian Church and Well Sites

When attempting to date the sites of ancient Welsh churches and holy wells we are faced with a number of difficulties. Does the Christian use of these sites actually extend back to the Age of the Saints? If a particular saint's name is attached to both a well and a nearby church is that proof that the saint founded the church and also made use of the well? Could it not be that both church and well were dedicated to that saint much later by an admiring follower? If that is the case then the dedication of that site would not be contemporary with the Age of the Saints. Indeed, the site may even have been dedicated to the saint during the later Middle Ages, at a time when the cult of the saints was being actively promoted on account of their 'Lives', which had become highly fashionable at that time.

A closer examination of some Llŷn church sites certainly suggests that they probably do date from the Age of the Saints, although it is possible that a few may have been dedicated to a particular saint some time after that saint's death. Many Llŷn churches are set within churchyards which are roughly circular or oval in plan, an indication, as Hilling stated, that they probably date from the early Christian period. A detailed examination of certain other Llŷn churchyards reveals that their perimeters were originally curviform but have been extended by the subsequent addition of rectangular plots of land. Furthermore, several church sites contain inscribed memorial stones dating from the 5th to the 7th century although we cannot be certain that, at some point in the past, some of those stones were not removed from their original positions before being re-located.

It is well documented that one or two Llŷn churches originally contained the actual tombs of saints. For example, written records suggest that the churches at Clynnog and Llanengan once contained the tombs of Saint Beuno and Saint Engan respectively, while an ancient inscription on a pillar within the church at Llangwnnadl records that it is the burial place of Saint Gwynhoedl. Furthermore, in the church at Abererch Manx pilgrims offered gifts at the shrine of Rhydderch Hael, a famous tribal leader from 'The Old North'. Tradition leads us to believe that Rhydderch had defeated a Northumbrian king in battle, thus saving the Isle of Man from almost certain invasion and subjection. As late as the 19th century there are accounts of Manx fishermen interrupting their fishing to go on pilgrimage to the church at Abererch to pay homage at the shrine of their hero.

The evidence outlined above, together with the sheer number of Llŷn churches which bear the names of Celtic saints, would suggest that many of them were founded by the early Christian saints themselves. It follows that, if a saint had established a church at a particular site, he would almost certainly have made use of the nearby holy well too.

Llŷn Christian Holy Wells during the Later Middle Ages

1. The Cult of the Holy Well during the Later Middle Ages

We have seen how the survival of the well-cult in Llŷn was actively promoted by the Celtic saints who took over and made use of some of the old pagan wells in the furtherance of their missionary work. Over time, this connection between the ancient wells of the peninsula and the Christian saints became extremely strong, and the significance of this association grew in popularity from the 11th century to the 16th century.

This was a time when the Church was one of the most powerful influences on people's lives. It provided a measure of stability and hope in a very uncertain world. The teachings of the Church gave meaning and structure to people's daily existence and it even controlled many of their thoughts and actions. The lives of the population were greatly influenced by the hope of salvation and by the fear of eternal damnation. There was a general belief that pleasing God and his saints during life on earth would bring lasting benefits in the 'after life'. And so, throughout the Later Middle Ages, as part of this relationship with God and his saints, rituals at Christian shrines and holy wells became extremely important.

During the latter half of this period some of those holy wells were enhanced by the addition of man-made stone structures, while well-shrines and well-chapels were built at or near to several springs. For hundreds of years holy wells continued to play an extremely important part in people's lives, right across Wales and indeed throughout Christendom.

It has already been mentioned that, although the whole of Britain including Wales was a Christian land, the period from

11th century onwards was a time when age-old superstitions were still commonplace, for belief in omens, portents, witches, spectres, goblins, monsters, physical demons and malevolent spirits resulted in the carving of hideous stone gargoyles and grotesques on the exterior of important religious buildings in order to guard against evil. In the 16th century, good luck objects were often attached to the external walls of people's dwellings to ward off devils and evil spirits. In many historic buildings, even those built as late as the 17th century, witches' marks and other protective graffiti were often cut into timbers, especially in roof spaces, and around doors, windows and fireplaces – in other words, in parts of the building which were considered to be particularly vulnerable to attack by evil spirits especially during the night. Good luck items of footwear were frequently hidden in chimneys and behind fireplaces right up to the middle years of the 19th century. (June Swann: 'Shoes concealed in buildings', 1996) The remains of a shoe were recently discovered behind a primitive range which had been built into the inglenook of an 18th century Nefyn cottage, probably during the mid 19th century.

The medieval concept of what might await a sinner after death is well illustrated by Dante's description of 'Inferno' in his epic poem 'Divine Comedy'. Here doomed souls are featured suffering horrific punishments for their sins on earth. The late 13th century Mappa Mundi in Hereford Cathedral illustrates, not only the physical world as it was perceived at that time, but also, above it, another world where Christ sits in judgement. Inside the gates of heaven the chosen ones are welcomed to paradise by the Virgin Mary accompanied by a group of angels, while a winged devil can be seen dragging sinners away to suffer eternally in Hell. Similarly, at a time when few people could read, the walls of many parish churches were adorned with large wall paintings, sometimes featuring terrifying pictorial representations of purgatory and doom. To this day such graphic representations can be seen in the churches at Chaldon (Surrey), Houghton-on-the-Hill (Norfolk) and Holy Trinity Church (Coventry). Therefore the lives of medieval people were profoundly influenced not only by the saints but also by other commonly accepted beliefs which caused them to reflect fearfully on what might ultimately await them after death.

Bearing all this in mind, it is not surprising that people considered it important to have someone on their side who could intercede for for them on Judgement Day. And who could be better equipped to do that than one of the saints? The 'Lives of the Saints', which were written down over a long period of time during the Later Middle Ages, led to a huge 'saint cult'. Right across the Christian world, people were more than happy to place their lives into the hands of God through the endeavours of his saints. This was a period during which the saints acquired celebrity status; their earthly remains were greatly revered; and shrines, often containing their relics, were set up in churches and cathedrals across the land. In Llŷn, Saint Beuno's shrine was said to have existed at Clynnog Fawr, and the tomb of Saint Engan (also known as Saint Einion) is said to have been visited in Llanengan church. Consequently both Llŷn churches became important local pilgrimage destinations in their own right. Statues of saints adorned the external walls of many religious buildings throughout the Christian world, and hordes of people from all walks of life flocked on pilgrimage to those shrines and wells which were most closely associated with their early Christian heroes. The saints had become the 'religious pop stars' of the Middle Ages.

Myths and legends about the saints and their wells evolved, and it was during the Later Middle Ages, hundreds of years after the saints themselves had died, that monks wrote down incredible stories about the lives of those early Christian figures. Such tales were readily believed and accepted, and, they became part and parcel of popular medieval Christian belief. Today we recognise that such stories are not historically accurate – indeed, they are the stuff of myth and legend. In the 1770s the traveller, Thomas Pennant, described one particular Llŷn legend about Saint Beuno and Saint Aelhaearn as '*too absurd to relate.*' Although we know that such tales are not factually true we must not, like Pennant, dismiss their significance out of hand, for they tell us a great deal about the times in which they were written and the effect that they had upon the minds and the lives of the ordinary people.

There are legends which tell of springs issuing forth from the ground where a saint had struck his staff (like the story of Saint Cybi at Llangybi), stories which are reminiscent of the Biblical story of Moses. Others tell of saints being decapitated by an evil adversary, and a well suddenly springing forth from the ground at the exact spot where the severed head of the saint had fallen. Other tales tell of saints restoring dead people back to life. All these legends were written down in order to glorify the lives of those early Christian saints and to further the cause of the Christian Church. Therefore the cult of the well was very closely linked to the veneration of the early Christian saints.

Although it does not relate directly to Llŷn, one of the most famous Welsh legends is that of Saint Winifred whose head, so the story says, was cut off by a young nobleman called Caradog after she had rebuffed his advances. It goes on to recount how a spring rose up from the ground on the exact spot where her severed head had landed, and in this way Saint Winifred's well at Holywell in Flintshire was born. Miraculously, according to the story, the saint's head was very quickly restored by her uncle, Saint Beuno, who then brought her back to life. The cult of Saint Beuno, of course, has very strong associations with Llŷn.

There is a similar legend concerning one of the holy wells in Llŷn, namely Ffynnon Ddigwig at Penarth near Clynnog Fawr. It states that Ffynnon Ddigwig was formed when a princess of the same name was decapitated by her young husband whom she had newly wed, and a spring suddenly emerged from the spot where her severed head had fallen. Once again, this story draws attention to the remarkable healing powers of Llŷn's most important saint, Beuno, who replaced the princess's head and restored her back to life.

Because legends like the ones concerning Ffynnon Ddigwig and Saint Winifred's well were accepted at their face value, medieval folk were convinced that those saintly heroes of old still had the power to influence their lives and heal their bodies. And so, on account of their associations with the early Celtic saints, many of the ancient wells of Llŷn were looked upon as extremely holy places. Stories which told of saints restoring people's health, resulted in many saints' wells beoming renowned for their healing qualities. The concept of the healing power of holy water, which was in evidence in Graeco-Roman and Romano-Celtic times, continued throughout the Later Middle Ages when, people were convinced that the water from a saint's holy well would be able to restore their diseased and injured bodies just as that saint had performed miraclulous cures during his or her life on earth.

It was probably towards the end of the Middle Ages, from the late 14th to the early 16th century, that the well-cult reached its height. The Royal Commission on Ancient and Historic Monuments in Wales has suggested that, where stone enhancements have been added to several of the peninsula's wells, certain of those features may be medieval in origin. Walls were built to enclose some important holy wells, and paving stones and steps were added so that the water could be more easily accessed. Effigies of the saints, placed in niches, adorned the walls of some holy wells. Ffynnon Beuno, at Clynnog Fawr, a few yards down the road from the site of Saint Beuno's monastery, is one such well. Many other Llŷn wells have also been identified as probable holy wells by the RCAHMW. To this day the water from certain holy wells in Llŷn is still used in local churches for holy baptism, as is the case with Ffynnon Fair at Bryncroes. (as stated by the vicar of Bryncroes) and Ffynnon Beuno at Clynnog Fawr (as recorded within Clynnog church).

2. Llŷn Wells and Medieval Pilgrimages

Certain other major world religions are also associated with pilgrimmage, for Muslims and Hindus also go on pilgrimage to holy sites. During the Middle Ages the Christian Church encouraged pilgrims to visit holy places, and the monetary gifts which they donated were plentiful. People believed that, if they prayed at a holy shrine or a saint's well and offered gifts, their sins would be forgiven and their illnesses would be cured. We have already seen how some Llŷn holy wells, such as those at Clynnog Fawr and Llanengan, became pilgrimage destinations in their own right. People visiting both of these places gratefully deposited their gifts of money into the large wooden chest or 'cyff' in grateful thanks for the saint's interventions on their behalf. Early wooden chests can still be seen inside the churches at both Clynnog and Llanengan. The rebuilding and extension of both those churches during the late 15th and early 16th centuries has produced buildings which now seem exceedingly grand for such small villages. Welsh people undertook pilgrimages to holy wells in large numbers, especially at the time of the 'gwylmabsant' or wake of the patron saint. It is said that these wakes were times of great rejoicing which frequently became extremely boisterous and rowdy occasions.

Holy wells were also very important places for people who were travelling on pilgrimage to the holy island of Ynys Enlli. At wells along the route the pilgrims could not only rest and refresh themselves but they could also obtain a blessing or seek a cure from the saint to whom the well was dedicated. Throughout the Later Middle Ages, right across Europe, people of all kinds, young and old, rich and poor, undertook pilgrimages. Even medieval monarchs went on pilgrimage. A few folk travelled to the Holy Land or to Rome, although the vast majority of pilgrims visited sites of great sanctity that were much nearer to home, especially those associated with local saints and their relics. In the 14th century the English poet Geoffrey Chaucer wrote about a group of people travelling on pilgrimage to the shrine of Saint Thomas Becket at Canterbury and the tales that they told as they journeyed.

Although some of the Llŷn wells were local pilgrim destinations the most important Welsh pilgrimage sites were Saint David's at the south-western extremity of the country, Saint Winifred's Well at Holywell in the north-eastern corner and the holy island of Ynys Enlli (*Bardsey*) at the tip of the Llŷn peninsula. Unlike Holywell and Saint David's, there was no single special shrine to attract people to Enlli. However, Enlli was revered and celebrated as the burial place of many of the important Celtic saints. An early source says of Ynys Enlli, 'Among the Welsh it is called the Welsh Rome because of the long and risky journey to the very end of the kingdom, and because of the holiness and purity of the place'. (*TCHS* No. 21)

Following his *Journey Through Wales* in the 12th century Gerald of Wales wrote, 'Beyond Lleyn there is a small island occupied by some extremely devout monks... Either because of its pure air, which comes across the sea from Ireland, or through some miracle occasioned by the merits of the holy men who live there, the island has this peculiarity, that no one dies there except in extreme old age, for disease is almost unheard of. In fact, no one dies there at all unless he is very old indeed... The bodies of a vast number of holy men are buried there.' (*Gerald of Wales*, Penguin Classics 2004 Edition)

Subsequently the island gained a reputation for being the final resting place of 20,000 saints, and as such, it was considered to be an extremely holy place. It must be remembered that important early Celtic Christian figures like Cadfan, Lleuddad, Deiniol, Dyfrig, and Cybi are believed to have been buried there. The island was considered to be so sacred that, after the Celtic and Roman Churches had joined together, the Pope issued a decree, declaring that three pilgrimages to Enlli were equal to one visit to Rome. Therefore, by the early sixteenth century, the tracks and the pathways of the peninsula were thronging with crowds of pilgrims as they wended their way towards the holy isle. But it was not only Welsh pilgrims who visited Enlli. Pilgrims from England also trekked westwards on pilgrimmage, for it is claimed that the village church at Tong in Shropshire was a 'pilgrim church' on the route to Enlli.

When pilgrims reached Llŷn, those approaching from the south would keep to the higher ground above Pentrefelin, pausing at Saint Ddunawd's Well to refresh themselves. Then they would make for Saint Cawrdaf's Church and well at Abererch. Moving on through Deneio, they would probably pause at Saint Pedrog's church and well in Llanbedrog and then Saint Einion's church and well at Llanengan. They would probably break the next stage of their journey at Saint Aelrhiw's well in Rhiw, before passing through Llanfaelrhys and then dropping down to the monastery at Aberdaron.

Pilgrims journeying from the north would call at Saint Deiniol's monastery at Bangor before proceeding to the abbey and well of Saint Beuno at Clynnog Fawr. Both Bangor and Clynnog were important gathering points for pilgrims journeying to Enlli from the north. Then they would make for Saint Aelhaearn's church and well at Llanaelhaearn. Another important stopping place was Pistyll, where travellers could not only seek a blessing or a cure at the holy well but they could also obtain accommodation, care and refreshment at the monastery and its hospice. The next stop would be the priory (before it lapsed in the 14th century) and well at Nefyn. Journeying via Edern, Tudweiliog and Penllech another stopping place was the church at Llangwnnadl which was originally established owing to the generosity of Gwynhoedl, a local chieftain who gave the land on which the church together with a small Christian community was established. Llangwnnadl church (where one of the pillars contains an inscription stating that Gwynhoedl is buried there) is believed to have contained the shrine of Saint Gwynhoedl, while a field next to the church is still referred to as Cae Eisteddfa (the field in which to rest), a name which harks back to the days when crowds of pilgrims visited and rested in this place. The church at Llangwnnadl was enlarged in 1520, a reflection of its importance as pilgrim church. Finally, on leaving Llangwnnadl, the pilgrims would head for the monastery at Aberdaron before crossing the Sound by boat to Ynys Enlli.

3. Well and Church Dedications during the Middle Ages

The dedication of wells and churches to the early local saints seems to have been a peculiarly Celtic Christian phenomenon, for they are particularly common in Wales and Cornwall but they fall away dramatically once we cross into the former

Anglo-Saxon parts of England. After the Edwardian conquest of Wales during the second half of the 13th century, a number of Llŷn holy wells were re-dedicated to Biblical saints and later Christian martyrs, although the majority continued to bear the names of early local Celtic saints.

It was the holy wells situated in the most important towns, where the Anglo-Norman influence was strongest, that tended to be re-dedicated. It was almost certainly during the Later Middle Ages that the well and the church at Cricieth (an Anglo-Norman medieval royal borough) were re-dedicated to Saint Catherine, the Middle Eastern saint and martyr – an unusual dedication in Wales.

The most common re-dedication of Welsh wells was to the Virgin Mary. Francis Jones has identified 76 Welsh wells that are dedicated to the Virgin Mary, although there are at least 5 others which he overlooked, including the well and church at Nefyn. Although the old Nefyn church has been rebuilt many times since the days of the saints, its raised churchyard, adjacent to the site of the former Celtic priory, undoubtedly suggests an ancient llan which dates back to the Age of the Saints when it must have been dedicated to a local saint.

But under the English crown Nefyn was a privileged settlement which had important associations with Anglo-Norman royalty. This town, which had been very important under the Princes of Gwynedd, now became one of the most important Anglo-Norman colonial towns in the shire. Since the Virgin Mary was the preferred saint of the Normans the church at Nefyn was re-dedicated as Llanfair yn Nefyn (the church of Mary in Nefyn). Similarly the town's well became known as Ffynnon Fair (*ffynnon*: well; *Fair*: Mary). Today, instead of being a place of worship, the old Saint Mary's Nefyn church is the Llŷn Maritime Museum which is excellent and well worth a visit, for it has been completely refurbished in recent years.

The old Nefyn well, which is now covered by a mid 19th century granite structure, is located just below Y Groes in the centre of the town.

Christian practices and beliefs surrounding holy wells continued to flourish in medieval Britain for nearly 500 years until Henry VIII and subsequent Protestant Tudor monarchs of the 16th century did their best to suppress them.

Well-Culture, the Protestant Reformation and the Rise of Nonconformity

1. The Protestant Reformation

During the 1500s the Protestant Reformation brought about a cataclysmic change in the affairs of Henry VIII's kingdom. For some time, the Roman Church had been criticised for its perceived abuses. In Germany Martin Luther had challenged the authority of the Pope as early as 1520. At that time King Henry VIII remained loyal to the Church in Rome, for in 1521 he supported the publishing of a document which attacked the teachings of Luther. He had also undertaken pilgrimages to the Holy Well at Walsingham in Norfolk and Saint Margaret's Well at Binsey in Oxfordshire. For his loyalty and piety the Pope bestowed upon him the title of 'Defender of the Faith'.

But the situation in Henry's kingdom changed dramatically when he declared his intention to divorce his queen, Katherine of Aragon, so that he could marry Anne Boleyn. The Pope was asked to give his blessing to the divorce but he refused. Consequently, Henry denounced the authority of the Pope and severed all ties between his kingdom and the Church in Rome. In 1534 the Protestant Reformation in Henry's kingdom was enshrined in law by the Act of Supremacy which recognised the English monarch as the sole and supreme Head of the Church of England.

Following this break with Rome, Thomas Cromwell, the king's Chief Minister and enforcer, undertook the task of consolidating the Reformation. He dissolved the extremely wealthy monasteries and abbeys, evicting the monks, destroying and ransacking their buildings, confiscating their riches and selling off or leasing their extensive and valuable lands.

Under succeeding Tudor monarchs, apart from Queen Mary I who was a Roman Catholic, efforts were made to suppress Catholicism and strengthen the Protestant Reformation. The persecution which followed was often brutal and, during the religious troubles of the Tudor period several religious martyrs (Catholic martyrs under Protestant monarchs and Protestant martyrs under Queen Mary I) were cruelly tortured and burnt at the stake. Trappings of the old religion found in cathedrals and parish churches were often removed or destroyed.

Many of the Pre-Reformation shrines were also demolished (including the 12th century shrine of Saint David at Saint David's in Pembrokeshire), as were many of the holy wells and the ancient chapels attached to them. Whilst the stonework of the wells and their chapels could be torn down, it was more difficult to destroy the water sources because they were natural springs. Although not all medieval holy wells were desecrated in this way, every effort was made to discourage people from visiting them. One elaborate Welsh holy well that escaped destruction was Saint Winifred's well at Holywell, a magnificent set of ornate buildings which had been erected in the early 1500s. It remains intact to this day.

The cult of saintly relics and religious pilgrimage, as well as the adoration of statues and crucifixes, so prevalent under Roman Catholicism were now forbidden, as were visits to wells and ancient shrines. Orders were issued that one particular Welsh well and chapel was to be completely destroyed 'not leaving one stone thereof upon an other' (cited by Jones: *The Holy Wells of Wales*). This directive also stated that any person found visiting 'by night or daie to the said chappell or well in superstitious manner' was to be detained and taken before the authorities.

In Llŷn, and indeed throughout Caernarfonshire, which was fairly remote from the centre of ecclesiastical power, the many religious changes brought about by the Henry VIII's Protestant Reformation were, for the most part, accepted as a matter of course. For many local people life and worship continued much the same as it had done before. At three large Llŷn houses, Penyberth, Plas Du and Maesog, the resident families clung to their Catholic faith, while small bodies of devout Catholics persisted within the peninsula although they were very small in percentage terms compared with the entire population.

Whilst most of the local clergy accepted the religious changes dispassionately, the poorer folk, who were neither well-educated nor well-informed about such matters, paid little attention to the changes and retained their old instincts and ways of life. The vast majority of people continued to worship in the local parish church as they had done previously and, in spite of official pronouncements from those in high authority, they continued to make their customary visits and pilgrimages to wells and shrines in large numbers. Leland stated that when he undertook his journey around Wales and England early in the 16th century Ffynnon Engan at Llanengan, Llŷn was still a place of pilgrimage for large numbers of people.

In 1576, during the reign of Elizabeth I, the Bishop of St. David's denounced from the pulpit those who 'defende papistrie, supersticion and Idolatrie, pilgrimages to Welles and blind Chappelles ...' (cited by Jones, *The Holy Wells of Wales*) A letter, dating from the late 16th century, stated that Welsh people 'doe still goe in heapes on pilgrimage to the wonted welles and places of superstition; and in the nights after the feastes when the ould offringes weare used to be kepte at anie chappell, albeit the church be pulled down, yet doe they come to the place where the church or chappell was by great jorneys barefoots.' (cited in *Arch. Camb*. Vol IV 6th Series) Therefore, in spite of the religious changes and the new orders issued by the Established Church, the rural poor of Wales continued to visit wells.

There is very little documentary evidence available about Llŷn well-sites at this time but a well-gathering at a mid-Wales well site was documented in 1595. On this occasion some of the people attending the well were apprehended and taken before the local magistrate, who was informed that approximately another two hundred people were still at the well but had not been arrested. This must have been a well pilgrimage in view of the large numbers of people involved. However, the magistrate refused to take any action, referring to those who had been brought before him as poor sickly folk who merely wished to wash themselves at the well, 'hoping by the help of God thereby to have their health.' (cited by Jones, *The Holy Wells of Wales*)

And so, whilst the majority of the clergy and certain other folk tended to toe the official line, in the more remote parts of the land the poor clung to their ancient traditions and kept the practice of well-visits very much alive.

2. The Attitude of the Puritans and the Dissenting Chapels towards Wells

The religious reforms of the Protestant Tudor monarchs had not moved fast enough for some people and so there emerged a new radical religious movement called Puritanism. This was a movement which embraced a militant, biblically-based brand of Protestantism, with the emphasis upon the removal, from both Church and Society, of all remaining traces of Roman Catholicsm. Initially the Puritans wished to purify the Established Church from within – hence the name 'Puritanism'. But the religious settlement of Elizabeth I's reign, in particular, had not been to the liking of the Puritans because they considered that the Church of England was being far too tolerant of practices associated with the old religion.

Over time, the Puritans became disillusioned with the Established Church and they began to distance themselves from it. Eventually the dissenting movement became more formalised and ultimately denominations like the Independents, the Presbyterians and the Baptists emerged.

In Llŷn, Puritanism prospered under the patronage of certain local gentry, especially the families of Nanhoron, Rhydolion, Castellmarch and Madryn; and from the second half of the 17th century onwards groups of Dissenters were active in Llŷn, especially in Pwllheli and in the parishes of Llangian and Llangybi. Naturally, since Puritans rejected the practices of the Roman Church, they viewed well-pilgrimages and well-practices as idolatry and superstition. Right across Wales Dissenters attacked visits to wells, for whatever purpose. In 1646 one Welsh critic issued this warning to the Welsh people, 'I need not remind thee of that swarm of blinde, superstitious ceremonies that are among us, passing under the name of old harmless custom; their frequent calling upon the saints in their prayers and blessings, their peregrinations to wells and chapels.' (cited by Jones, *The Holy Wells of Wales*)

But in spite of such exhortations, the ancient customs and practices of the ordinary folk continued, although by this time the majority of Llŷn well-visits tended to be solely for the purpose of healing which, of course, was also vigorously condemned. Both the Established Church and the leading Dissenters looked upon well visits as tantamount to witchcraft. Nevertheless, some Llŷn wells continued to be improved and added to, as was the case with Ffynnon Fair at Bryncroes. Here, a stone basin was constructed to hold the well water, walls were built around the basin and stone steps were added to facilitate ease of access to the pool – probably in the 17th century according to the RCAHMW.

Throughout the 18th century the Established Church in Wales fell into a decline. This coincided with rise of Methodism, especially Calvinistic Methodism, a denomination which was to become a highly vocal opponent of the practices associated with the Catholic Church. The Calvinistic Methodists were influenced greatly by the writings and preaching of a 16th century, Geneva-based, French-born theologian called John Calvin. Like Luther in Germany, Calvin had denounced the Catholic Church in France. Having fled to Switzerland, he had produced his own blueprint for a personal religious faith and a simpler, scripture-based form of worship, which he maintained would regenerate the world spiritually. Over time his teachings spread right across Europe.

From the first half of the nineteenth century onwards Calvinistic Methodism grew at an incredible rate across Caernarfonshire, and by 1851 it had become the dominant religious denomination within the county. Very strict religious views prevailed amongst the Calvinistic leaders so that all superstitious practices, including well-pilgrimages, well-gatherings and their associated rituals, were denounced as ungodly.

As early as 1801 the Calvinistic Methodist leadership published their Rules of Discipline which stated that none of their members 'should practice magic or witchcraft for personal gain upon man or beast; or follow sorcerers; or seek out magicians or make offerings to wells; or follow any corrupt practice of this kind; or consult devils.'

There was also a note which stated: 'Charming (or as some say 'counting') warts or cancers or any other ailment, what is that but consulting the Devil as a doctor? Making sacrifices to Ffynnon Eilian (or any other well) for our own benefit or for that of our livestock, or attempting to avenge ourselves upon somebody, what is that but making a sacrifice to the Devil and calling upon his fiendish assistance? These customs are very common in some parts of our country; shame upon their blind, ignorant and ungodly inhabitants.' Ieuan Lleyn, the Bryncroes-born schoolmaster and poet whose maternal grandfather, Siarl Marc, was a leading Llŷn Nonconformist preacher, dismissed many of the old Pre-Reformation religious traditions as 'relics of Popery'.

But once again, despite this hostility, many of the ancient and firmly-entrenched folk practices refused to go away, and people continued to visit wells. It seems that the ordinary members of the chapel congregations saw no contradiction between their Calvinistic faith and their superstitious beliefs and practices.

A Changing Attitude towards Wells Emerges in the 18th & 19th Centuries

During the 18th and 19th centuries, despite the views of the Nonconformist leaders, certain writers became increasingly interested in antiquities and folklore, including the culture surrounding wells. The Enlightenment, an intellectual, cultural and social movement which emphasised the importance of reason, analysis, individuality and independent thinking rather than the authoritarianism and superstition of the Middle Ages, brought about a changing attitude. The seeds of this change had been sown in the late 17th century when Welsh authors like Edward Lhuyd had begun to write about Welsh antiquities. Later on, the practice was continued by other writers who travelled the Welsh countryside, noting things of interest, including tales about the ordinary folk and their customs.

The 18th century, sometimes referred to as the 'Age of Reason', was an age of intellectual curiosity, medical advancement, scientific observation and experiment. Certain ancient wells were now accepted, often on expert authority, as genuine places of healing. The waters from these wells were analysed scientifically in order to verify their healing properties. In certain cases landowners capitalised on their good fortune and turned their springs into health-enhancing spas. Certain Welsh place names, like Builth Wells, Llandrindod Wells and Llanwrtyd Wells are evidence of the discovery during the 17th and 18th centuries of the health-giving natural spring waters at those places, although they did not become fashionable spa resorts until Victorian times when the term 'Wells' attached to their place names.

In Llŷn, during the mid-18th century, Ffynnon Gybi, the holy well at Llangybi, achieved considerable notoriety as a place of healing. Having received a favourable scientific report concerning the healing properties of its well water, the landowner decided to turn Ffynnon Gybi into a small health spa. He constructed additional buildings and facilities on the site and employed a well-keeper to look after it. The news of this well spread, and soon people from the surrounding area and far beyond were flocking to bathe in its water and to partake of its curative properties. Many people carried containers of the virtuous water away with them so that their treatment could be continued at home.

Throughout the 18th century and early 19th century, in spite of the influences of the Enlightenment, many of the rural poor still believed in the healing power of the ancient saints like Beuno. Consequently sick and infirm folk continued to travel considerable distances to visit the wells and shrines associated with the old saints in order to obtain a cure for their illnesses and disabilities. This is illustrated by Pennant's account of what he witnessed at the church in Clynnog Fawr in the 1770s. There he saw a 'poor paralytic' from Merionethshire who was seeking a cure for his condition. The disabled patient had first been carried to Saint Beuno's holy well where he was lifted bodily into the well water to bathe. Then he was carried down the road to Saint Beuno's church where he spent the night, sleeping on a feather mattress which had been placed on top of the saint's tomb.

As the 19th century progressed, with the development of popular education, the improvement in medical science and a greater interest in folk culture, a different view of wells began to take root. Some people were now viewing such features simply as interesting survivals from a bygone age. The

Topographical Dictionaries of Wales produced by Nicholas Carlisle (1811) and Samuel Lewis (1843) contain several references to wells, while articles published in early editions of *Archaeologia Cambrensis* include information about a number of Welsh well-sites. Elias Owen, Welsh cleric and antiquary, was engaged in writing a book about the 'Holy Wells of North Wales' but he died in May 1899 before he was able to finish it. His unfinished manuscript is housed in the National Library of Wales.

Although the majority of Welsh rural folk continued to hold fast to their traditional beliefs and practices, those who were motivated by conviction continued to see well-rituals as anti-Christian sorcery. Alternatively, there were others who were now viewing wells as an important part of the nation's folklore which was worthy of academic study. And so during the second half of the 19th century, as Francis Jones points out, in academic circles 'the scholarship of 'folklore' began to supersede the stigma of superstition'. (Jones: *The Holy Wells of Wales*)

The Folklore Society was founded in 1878 to encourage the collection and recording of folklore. The study of Welsh folk culture became so fashionable during the later years of the 19th century that there were even Welsh folklore competitions at eisteddfodau, including the National Eisteddfod of Wales. There developed a renewed academic interest in the lives of the saints and their connections with wells and megaliths. *The Lives of the Saints* was published in 1907 by Baring-Gould and Fisher, and The Royal Commission on the Ancient and Historical Monuments of Wales was founded in 1908. Both will be mentioned from time to time in Part II of this book.

An important source of information about the folklore of Llŷn is John Jones (1836-1921), a Llŷn-born writer and antiquarian who is better known by his bardic name, Myrddin

Fardd. Born at Tan-y-Ffordd in the parish of Llangian, he was a blacksmith by trade, working in various local smithies and quarries. Fascinated by the local history and folklore of Llŷn, he was a regular competitor at eisteddfodau and he published several books. His book *Llên Gwerin Sir Gaernarfon*, published in 1908, is a mine of information about the folklore and wells of the area. During his lifetime he explored many of the peninsula's wells and ancient churchyards; he talked to aged villagers and wrote down their recollections; and he collected snippets of Llŷn history and numerous tales about the peninsula. Without his efforts much of our knowledge about the beliefs and practices associated with Llŷn wells would have been lost for ever.

On more than one occasion Myrddin Fardd met Sir John Rhŷs (1840-1915), a distinguished Celtic scholar and a leading antiquarian. Like Myrddin Fardd he came from humble beginnings, but he had risen to become Professor of Celtic Studies at Jesus College, Oxford. He, too, took a keen interest in Welsh antiquities and folklore, and for a time he served as Chairman of the Commission on Ancient Monuments in Wales. It was Sir John Rhŷs, more than any other academic, who raised the study of Welsh folklore to the status of scholarship. In his chapter on 'The Folklore of the Wells' Sir John describes the rituals observed at a number of Llŷn wells, although he makes it clear that he had obtained quite a lot of his information from a local man – Myrddin Fardd.

As far as the majority of Llŷn villagers were concerned, although much of the ancient well-culture had ceased to be practised by start of the 20th century, many long-standing Llŷn superstitions about ghosts, fairies, mythical creatures and strange supernatural happenings continued to hold sway. When writing his book *Llên Gwerin Sir Gaernarfon* in 1908 Myrddin Fardd was very well aware of this, for he wrote of the peninsula, 'Some ghost lives at the foot of every hedge, a dead man's candle lights every church, a white lady watches over every crossroads, and spectres are as frequent as gorse bushes ...'

The Demise of the Old Llŷn Well Culture and a Resurgence of Interest in the History of Wells

It is not clear exactly when traditional folk practices ceased to be observed at Llŷn wells. Age-old rituals were certainly still being practised at wells in other parts of Wales as late as the early part of the 20th century. It is recorded by Francis Jones that, at one Pembrokeshire well, people drank holy water from a saint's skull during the 1914-18 war in the hope that their actions would bring about an early end to the hostilities. Apparently, as late as 1945, one Llŷn well was visited by the members of a Birmingham family as they sought help from its remarkable powers, but such a visit was extremely unusual by the mid 20th century. (See section on Ffynnon Fyw in Part II).

We can be fairly certain that during the 20th century, which brought with it two devastating World Wars, a National Health Service and a changed way of life, the ancient Llŷn well-culture had virtually died out. Nevertheless, the old wells were not finished. Many Llŷn wells remained important because they continued to supply domestic water to villages and isolated dwellings until the late 1950s when piped water was finally brought to the whole of Llŷn. Once the Cwm Ystradllyn reservoir scheme had been completed there was no longer the same need for the old natural wells, and therefore many of them became neglected and overgrown, while some were destroyed as a result of drainage schemes, agriculture and building work.

In more recent times there has been a revival of interest in the history of ancient wells and the Celtic tradition. Today more and more people are hankering after the simplicity and spirituality of the lives lived by the Celtic saints. Amidst the hustle, bustle and confusion of life in the 21st century they are heeding the advice offered in the Book of Jeremiah: 'Ask for the old paths and you will find rest for your souls.'

During the 20th century the Church in Wales re-emphasised its links with the Celtic saints and the pilgrims of old. In 1950 and again in 1992 thousands of Llŷn people, led by the Bishop of Bangor, undertook 20th century pilgrimages from Clynnog Fawr to Ynys Enlli, as they followed the northern pilgrim route in a convoy of cars. In 2011 the Bishop of Bangor re-consecrated Ffynnon Dudwen, an ancient Llŷn holy well which had recently been restored. In the 21st century thousands of people continue to be inspired as they walk the old pilgrim routes, just as folk used to do hundreds of years ago. During the summer of 2014 a 130 mile North Wales Pilgrim Route stretching from Saint Winifred's Well in Flintshire to Ynys Enlli was officially opened. It includes some of the most beautiful scenery in Wales as well as numerous historic sites including ancient churches and pilgrim wells.

The back cover of Elizabeth Rees's book *Celtic Saints and their Landscape* contains this paragraph, 'With its emphasis on the persuasiveness of the divine in the world around us .... Celtic Christianity appeals to the present day purity of spirit in a tarnished civilisation. .... The sites where Celtic monks, nuns and missionary couples lived and worked can still be seen in the more remote parts of Britain. Their huts, holy wells and chapels are often set in beautiful landscapes; sheltered valleys, dramatic headlands and rocky islands.' Of nowhere is this statement more appropriate than Llŷn, which still resonates with the lives of the early Celtic saints who, many centuries ago, brought the Christian gospel to this corner of northwestern Wales.

The Names of Llŷn Wells

The names of the ancient wells of Llŷn are interesting. We have seen that many Llŷn wells are named after the early Celtic saints who came to the peninsula to spread the Christian gospel. We have also noted that a few holy wells, probably originally dedicated to Celtic saints, were subsequently re-dedicated to Biblical and later saints, such as the Virgin Mary or Saint Catherine. Several wells have been given other names which point to their religious connections – wells like Ffynnon Saint, Ffynnon Sanctaidd (*sanctaidd*: holy), Ffynnon Fyw (*holy well*) or Ffynnon Dduw (*Duw*: God).

One or two wells are identified by the titles or names of lay people e.g. Ffynnon y Brenin (*brenin*: king), Ffynnon Grasi (Grace) and Ffynnon John Morgan. It was not unusual for wells to be named after creatures, as is the case with Ffynnon Sarff (*sarff*: serpent) and Ffynnon Defaid (*defaid*: sheep or warts). Several others bear the names of the topographical features of the landscape in which they are situated e.g. Ffynnon Pant (hollow) and Ffynnon Cae Garw (rough field). One well in Mynytho has a name which either denotes the sparkling purity of its water or its association with treasure – Ffynnon Arian (*arian*: silver or money). There are also wells which have taken the geographical names of the localities in which they are situated (Ffynnon Penllech, Ffynnon Mynydd Nefyn and Ffynnon Saethon) while one or two are named after nearby buildings (Ffynnon Tyddyn Iolyn, Ffynnon Tŷ Mawr and Ffynnon Felin Bach).

Unfortunately, it is probable that the ancient names of many natural wells have been completely lost in the mists of time. One well near Aberdaron was discovered during the late

20th century during road-widening and, although nobody knew its original name, the inhabitants of the village created a modern name for it (see the Inventory in Part II of this book).

Different Uses of Wells in Llŷn

It was stated earlier in this book that the wells of Llŷn were used for a variety of purposes and that individual wells became renowned for specific functions. Clearly, the most basic function was to supply fresh water, and as we have seen already, for thousands of years the natural wells of Llŷn were used for that purpose. Initially, in the main towns of Llŷn, those water sources were simply open wells, just as nature created them, although hand pumps were subsequently fitted to some. It was not until the later years of the 19th century, following several serious outbreaks of water-borne diseases, that piped water was finally provided in Porthmadog (1870), Pwllheli (1879) and Cricieth (1883). Nevertheless, despite the dangers, some townspeople still preferred to use natural wells rather than to pay for piped water.

In Nefyn, until 1906, the sole source of water for the inhabitants was Ffynnon Fair, when a small reservoir was constructed above the town on Mynydd Nefyn by the 'Lleyn Rural District Council'. However, people living in numerous small Llŷn villages throughout the peninsula still continued to carry water from natural wells until the reservoir at Cwm Ystradllyn was opened in 1959. Older Llŷn residents can remember how farmers were forced to carry water from natural springs to supply not only their families but also their livestock. Documentary evidence records that in some parts of Llŷn many wells dried up during prolonged periods of drought, requiring people to walk many extra miles in order to fetch water from springs which were still flowing.

But, of course, over many centuries, some Llŷn wells had gained reputations for possessing extraordinary powers. We have seen how many local holy wells were revered as places where people could obtain blessings from the saints to whom they are dedicated. Therefore, it is not surprising that the water from a number of holy wells should have been used regularly in local churches during Christian rituals. The water from Ffynnon Gadfarch at Abererch, Ffynnon Beuno at Clynnog, Ffynnon Fair at Bryncroes, Ffynnon Sanctaidd at Pistyll and one of the Carnguwch wells was used for baptisms. At one time, whenever there was a baptism at Abererch Church the well water was carried more than 2 miles from Ffynnon Gadfarch which was at the most northerly end of the parish. At another Llŷn church it was the custom every Sunday to sprinkle the members of the congregation with holy well water at the church door as they entered the building for worship.

Many other wells on the peninsula achieved notoriety for treating various illnesses, although the ailments which the well water was reputed to be able to cure differed from well to well. For centuries, before the advance of medical science, a visit to a holy well or the application of a plant remedy were the commonly accepted ways of treating illnesses. Such methods were usually based upon long-established tradition or superstition. As Francis Jones discovered, Caernarfonshire has far more healing wells than any other Welsh county and many of those wells were still being used to treat people's ailments into the 19th century.

The complaints which Llŷn wells were thought to be able to cure included fainting fits, warts, boils, gout, toothache, rheumatism, stomach problems, bowel conditions, eye complaints, skin ailments, scrofula, scurvy, gangrene, depression, epilepsy and infertility. The treatment usually consisted of either drinking some of the well water or bathing in it – or a combination of both. Sometimes local farmers took their sick livestock to local wells to be treated, and one or two Llŷn wells were alleged to be able to cure any kind of ailment in both man and beast. Because of its curative powers the waters from Ffynnon Saint at Aberdaron, when mixed with white heather honey and gorse flowers, was used to make a medicine which was said to be excellent for the treatment of depression.

We may wonder if the water from some Llŷn wells really did contain effective healing properties. It is not difficult to accept that certain wells, where the water was high in trace elements which had been absorbed from the rocks over which the water had flowed, may have been able to improve specific medical conditions. For example, the water from two Llŷn wells contained such an unusually high iron content that they were found to be particularly effective for the treatment of anaemia. Neither is it difficult to accept that some cool well waters may have been able to soothe tired eyes and aching limbs.

In respect of the more serious complaints, however, it is perhaps more likely that a person's cure from his or her condition stemmed from that person's absolute faith in the healing properties of the water, in the same way that a placebo can sometimes appear to bring about a marked improvement in a condition. As we shall see in due course, the healing wells of Llŷn were many, and some were considered to be both healing wells and holy wells.

In times past, wells were also used for a variety of other purposes. Until relatively modern times it was commonly believed that certain Llŷn wells had the power to foretell and influence the future. For example, there were wells on the peninsula which were reputed to be able to confirm the name of a thief, while others were often visited by lovers seeking favourable signs or ill omens about their romantic relationships. Ffynnon Dudwen was sometimes visited by local farmers in the hope that Saint Tudwen would increase the yield of their crops.

On the other hand, Ffynnon Arian at Mynytho is remembered simply as a wishing or good luck well. There are tales of clandestine marriages being performed at Ffynnon Dudwen, and in other parts of Wales there were also malignant wells which could be used for placing a curse upon one's enemies – hardly the most Christian reason for visiting a well one would have thought!

Some ancient springs were notable landmarks within the landscape. Sometimes they are mentioned in old documents either as boundary markers at the extremity of parishes or to pinpoint specific dwellings. The waters flowing away from the holy wells at Llanaelhaearn and Rhiw were used to power small local mills.

Traditional Practices Carried out at Llŷn Wells

There were numerous traditional practices associated with the old wells of Llŷn, and those rituals varied greatly from well to well. It was customary to visit certain wells on specific days; for example, it was the tradition to visit Ffynnon Saint at Cricieth every Easter Day while Ffynnon Saint on Mynydd y Rhiw was traditionally visited on Ascension Day. It is said that the young ladies of the Llangybi area used to gather at Ffynnon Gybi on Saint Cybi's Day. In the Middle Ages, on the feast of a particular saint, it was the common practice for people to go on pilgrimage to the well which was dedicated to that saint. There were wells where it was necessary to approach from a particular direction or to perform a specified ritual. At one or two wells it was considered essential to kneel in front of the well and to profess one's faith to the water. At other wells people simply had to kneel before the well and offer a prayer.

Frequently it was considered necessary to offer gifts at holy wells. As we saw earlier in this book the practice of offering gifts at wells goes back to the Bronze Age and Romano-Celtic times. The offering of gifts is still reasonably common in some Catholic countries, like the Irish Republic, where ribbons, rosaries and other small gifts can sometimes be seen tied to trees near Irish holy wells in remembrance of and in tribute to the saints. In the recent past coins, dressmakers' pins and even the thorns from a hawthorn tree were thrown into Llŷn wells as offerings and, during the early 20th century, large numbers of pins were found in a black stone container at Ffynnon Bedrog at Llanbedrog. Frequently the pins were bent before casting them into the well which is reminscent of the well-offerings made by the Bronze Age and Iron Age peoples who deposited bent and broken hand-crafted metal objects into the water to honour or appease their gods – an indication that such practices at Christian holy wells harked back to the days of the ancient tribes. At another Llŷn well, Ffynnon Ddigwig, it was customary to offer eggs as well as pins. At Ffynnon Gybi, in order to bring about a cure, visitors were required to throw pennies and silver coins into the well after bathing.

Although it was a Roman custom to throw pins into wells as offerings, initially in Llŷn it is likely that the thorns of a hawthorn tree were gathered and cast into the water as gifts, for manufactured pins were not commonly available in Wales before the Industrial Revolution. Myrddin Fardd reminds us that the offering of hawthorns used to be a common practice at Llŷn wells which would seem to confirm that there was a long standing connection in the peninsula between hawthorn trees and holy wells.

At healing wells the ritual differed from well to well. A procedure to banish warts involved piercing each wart with a pin and then casting the pin into the well water. It was necessary to use a different pin for each wart, and at some wells it was essential to bend the pin before throwing it into the water, a tradition reminiscent of the Iron Age practice of breaking and bending metal gifts before casting them into the water.

Sir John Rhŷs tells us that an entrant to the 'Folklore of North Wales Competition' at the National Eisteddfod held in London in 1887 described a ritual for curing warts which involved pins and sheep's wool. According to the competitor, in order to achieve a cure for his warts he had to look for some sheep's wool so that each wart could be pricked with a pin and then rubbed with the wool. Next, the pin had to be bent and thrown into the well. Finally, he had to hang the sheep's wool on a nearby hawthorn tree, for it was believed that, as the wool was scattered by the wind, so the warts would disappear.

This National Eisteddfod competitor went on to state that there was a well of this type near his home. He stated that one day he, and three or four other boys, went to the well after school to charm their warts away, for the writer had twenty-three such disfigurements on one of his hands. He states that he could not remember what happened to the other boys, but his own warts disappeared soon after undergoing this treatment. He stated that his grandfather firmly attributed the disappearance of his warts to the virtue of the well water (incident recorded by Sir John Rhys in his *Folklore of Wales*).

At healing wells it was sometimes considered necessary to leave pieces of rag behind after a visit, as was the practice at Ffynnon Cefn Lleithfan. The ailing or injured person would go to the well with a rag or clout tied around the particular part of the body which required treatment. On reaching the well the rag would be dipped into the well water and then used to bathe the affected body part. Once this treatment had been completed, the rag would be hung on the branch of a nearby hawthorn tree or pushed into the stonework surrounding the well in the belief that, as the piece of rag rotted, so the disease or injury would disappear from the body.

The ritual of leaving pieces of rag at well sites has been found fairly recently at certain well-sites in other parts of Britain where they were discovered festooning the branches of nearby trees. Such a scene was observed during the late 20th century at a Cornish well-site by Ted Harrison, a former BBC religious correspondent. At one Llŷn well, once the bathing had been completed, the piece of rag had to be pushed under the large stone which formed the threshold at the well entrance or pushed between stones in the well wall. In his book Sir John Rhŷs mentioned that he had often seen rags pushed under stones at well entrances or thrust into holes in the well walls although, at that time, he had no idea how they came to be there.

Certain Llŷn wells were believed to possess the power of prophecy. Some were famous for being able to foretell a sick person's future. At some prophetic wells the patient's garment was thrown into the water, and the outcome was interpreted according to whether the garment floated or sank. If the garment floated the signs were good, but if it sank the predicted outcome was death. Other prophecies were sought by casting handkerchiefs, feathers or hawthorns into the water. The prophecy could be read according to which part of the well basin those items drifted.

Other wells were considered capable of revealing the identity of a thief. The aggrieved person would go the well carrying pieces of bread. Each time he or she recited the name of one of the suspects on the list a piece of bread would be cast into the water. If the piece of bread floated the suspect whose name had been mentioned was innocent. This process was repeated until one of the pieces of bread sank to the bottom in which case the culprit had been found. The practice of casting 'bread in a spring' is denounced in the letter written by Saint Martin of Braga in the 6th century although the context of that Celtic tradition is not explained. However, since this practice is specifically mentioned at such an early period, it must have been part of an ancient Dark Age practice.

Certain wells were renowned for putting curses on enemies. It is known that the Romans used wells for this purpose, for numerous tablets of tin and lead have been found in Celtic wells with Roman curses scratched onto them. In more recent times the practice was also common at certain Welsh wells and Janet Bord explains that there was a rigid procedure laid down for putting a curse on someone. At one Welsh well it was necessary to write the name of the person being cursed on a piece of paper, before fastening it to a stone and casting it into the well. At another Welsh cursing well pieces of slate with people's initials scratched on them have been found in the water.

The effects of a well curse could be devastating for the victim, even life-changing. In one case, documented by Elias Owen, a young man was cursed for a previous love affair. He was told that the curse would not harm him as long as he remained within the four walls of his house. He was so determined to avoid the effects of the curse that he followed the advice implicitly. Eventually he died a bachelor in old age without ever having set foot outside the door of his home again.

It was a common belief that certain wells were guarded by creatures which lived in the water. As its name suggests, Ffynnon Sarff was alleged to have been guarded by a resident serpent, while eels were reputed to have lived in the wells at Ffynnon Gybi and Dyno Goch on Ynys Enlli. Some people maintained that they had seen such creatures in those wells, and it was commonly believed that the treatment would only prove effective if the well guardian was present. At one time there was an uproar in the village of Llangybi when a rumour was spread around the neighbourhood that the resident eel had been caught and removed from the well. Local people were convinced that the removal of the eel had destroyed the virtue of the well water.

There was also a traditional belief in Llŷn that fairies and elves gathered secretly at certain well-sites, as for example at Ffynnon Dalar on Ynys Enlli. Ghost stories and treasure tales are also associated with one or two Llŷn wells. For example, Ffynnon Grasi at Glasfryn is associated with a fairy story and a ghost story, while both a treasure story and a ghost story are linked to Ffynnon Ddigwig, near Clynnog Fawr. These stories are narrated in the appropriate sections of the Inventory of Wells in Part II of this book. Francis Jones suggests that, on account of its name, Ffynnon Arian (the wishing well at Mynytho) may originally have been connected to a treasure story, although this seems to be pure conjecture on his part.

At certain times of the year two Llŷn wells became places of great merriment and recreation. It is recorded by two separate writers, one in the 18th century and the other in the early 19th century, that Ffynnon Fyw (Mynytho) was the scene of great merriment on certain Sundays each summer when large numbers of people would gather there to play ball games and rustic sports. It is also documented that, during the 19th century, there was great rejoicing and boisterous merry-making at Ffynnon Gybi on Saint Cybi's feast day. These recreational activities may have been relics of the religious wakes which used to be held at holy well-sites on saints' feast days during the Middle Ages when it is recorded that there was great revelry and noisy behaviour among the revellers

Holy Wells?

We have seen that many of the ancient wells of Llŷn are referred to as 'holy' wells, but can they really be considered to be 'holy'? There appears to be some confusion surrounding this terminology. If certain wells are to be considered 'holy' what is it that affords them their sanctity? Some historians, like James Rattue, argue that it is not only wells connected with the early Christian saints that should be looked upon as holy but also wells associated with the pagan deities of the pre-Christian era. Whilst it is not difficult to understand the thinking behind such a suggestion there is a problem with it – we simply do not know for certain which wells were used as pagan sacred sites by the ancient tribes because we do not have the necessary evidence.

Other authors state that all wells which were considered to possess supernatural powers should be classified as holy wells. In his book *The Holy Wells of Wales,* Francis Jones certainly includes details of all such named wells, including saints' wells, healing wells, wells of prophecy, cursing wells, wishing wells, treasure wells and fairy wells. Clearly some of these wells do not deserve to be afforded the title 'holy'. Fairy wells and treasure wells were frequently so called on account of the age-old superstitions and ancient legends attached to them. More importantly, although cursing wells were clearly thought to possess extraordinary supernatural powers, surely it would be inappropriate for us to refer to them as 'holy' wells! That would seem to be a contradiction in terms for there is nothing holy about placing a curse upon another person! However, it has to be acknowledged that some wells which are known to have been used for prophecy or cursing may once have been holy wells, and that their religious associations may have been lost over time.

Because of the difficulties outlined above the criteria used by the author to define holy wells are as follows:

1. those wells which are dedicated by name to a particular saint, as well as those which include terms such as Saint, God, Trinity or Holy etc. in their titles.
2. those wells which are located adjacent to places of worship.
3. those wells which were visited by pilgrims because they were associated with healing and offerings.

The above definitions are similar to those adopted by Dyfed Archaeological Trust in their survey of Dyfed wells. Other ancient wells are simply referred to as wishing wells, wells of prophecy, treasure wells, fairy wells and cursing wells.

The Future of Our Ancient Wells

People may ask, 'Why should we study and seek to preserve our ancient wells?' The answer is simple – they are an important and interesting aspect of our cultural past. We have seen how many of these ancient natural springs afford us clues about how our ancestors lived before the dawn of recorded history. When we visit wells we may be looking at ancient religious sites where, thousands of years ago, pagan peoples performed their sacred rituals. At one time such practices must have been extremely common, not only throughout Wales and the whole of Britain, but right across the continental Europe. We can also appreciate the part that these springs played in the missionary work of the pioneering Celtic saints who first introduced Christianity to this part of Wales.

By studying these historic water features we can learn much about the beliefs and practices associated with them and the ancient folklore which sprang up around them. Therefore, along with all other historic features of the landscape, wells form an important part of our heritage, for they provide small windows through which we can glimpse the past. Also important are the old names of wells, the accounts written about them and the legends associated with them.

Whilst such documentary material is recorded safely in books and archives, unfortunately many of the wells themselves are not so secure. Over time, after superstitious belief had waned, after the National Health Service had been created to take care of people's ill health, and after all communities on the peninsula had been provided with piped water, the natural wells ceased to be an essential part of people's daily lives. Subsequently some were simply destroyed, while many others, owing to neglect, disappeared beneath masses of vegetation and were forgotten.

But all is not doom and gloom. In recent years there has been a growing awareness of, and interest in, the ancient wells of Llŷn, and indeed of historic Welsh wells generally. A few local wells, including Ffynnon Gybi at Llangybi, Ffynnon Fair at Nefyn, Ffynnon Engan at Llanengan, have been afforded 'Listed Building Status' while the establishment of societies like Cymdeithas Ffynhonnau Cymru (The Wells Society of Wales) and the Wellsprings Fellowship – two organisations dedicated to pin-pointing, promoting and preserving Welsh wells – is indicative of the growing interest in such sites.

In Gwynedd, within the Llŷn Area of Outstanding Natural Beauty, the AONB team has attempted to identify, visit and assess as many of the ancient wells as possible. Consequently several Llŷn wells, which were in danger of being lost altogether, have recently been rediscovered and recorded. Furthermore, as a result of the efforts of this group, and supported by landowners, local authorities and Gwynedd County Council, a few of the most important wells on the peninsula, like Ffynnon Aelhaearn, Ffynnon Aelrhiw, Ffynnon Dudwen, Ffynnon Engan, Ffynnon Fyw and Ffynnon Saint at Aberdaron were cleared of vegetation and renovated during the early years of the 21st century. Ffynnon Gybi, which is in the care of CADW, is very well looked after, while Ffynnon Fair at Nefyn, is in the guardianship of the Nefyn Town Trust.

Nevertheless, despite the renewed interest in our ancient wells many of them remain under threat. Clearly, it is those examples which have been enhanced by the addition of some kind of man-made superstructure that are most likely to survive and be preserved.

It is to be hoped that, in the future, many more of our historic wells will be refurbished, for there is now a growing recognition that they add greatly to the general character of the area since they are of interest not only to many local inhabitants but also to some of the visitors who come to Llŷn. There is however a recurring problem – shortly after work has been carried out at a well-site the vegetation invades again, and the spring soon disappears from view once more under a profusion of weeds and brambles.

Summary

We can see that, over thousands of years, the cult of the natural well or spring has had a chequered existence. We know that numerous springs were present in the peninsula long before Christianity arrived on the peninsula because they are natural features of the landscape. We can readily accept that many of those natural wells must have been used by the earliest Llŷn inhabitants as sources of drinking water, but some were almost certainly also considered extremely important as the dwelling places of water deities, for there is a long tradition of people worldwide worshipping water gods in springs, lakes and rivers. Some Llŷn wells were almost certainly used for religious purposes by the Dark Age pagan inhabitants of this area.

Since Roman Christianity did not reach the Iron Age tribes of Llŷn, it was left to the early Celtic missionary saints to bring the Christian gospel to these parts. Many of those saints built their churches close to the natural springs which had been sacred to the Celts. They blessed those wells in the service of God and made use of them in their evangelising missions. Wherever a saint settled he invariably gave his name not only to the llan and church which he established but also to the nearby well. In this way it was not only the Llŷn churches that became holy Christian places but also some of the peninsula's ancient wells.

Throughout the Middle Ages the cult of the well continued to be very important in the lives of the people. Some were considered to be holy wells and many were also renowned for their healing properties. Certain holy wells became places of pilgrimage in their own right while others were important stopping places on the medieval pilgrim route to Ynys Enlli. At holy wells the pilgrims could not only refresh themselves and seek the saint's blessing but they could also obtain a cure for an illness. In time, some wells and springs were enhanced by the addition of stone walls, basins and seats as well as paved walkways. Traditional practices and rituals were associated with many wells, and an abundance of stories and legends sprang up around them. Over hundreds years the reputations of holy wells were enhanced and during the Middle Ages they became integral to the cult of the saints. Holy wells became an important part of medieval Christian belief and practice.

During the religious upheaval of the Reformation, and the subsequent rise of Puritanism and religious Nonconformity, efforts were made to banish everything associated with Roman Catholicism – all superstitious belief, its form of worship, and the cult surrounding wells. Eventually, as the importance of the old religion waned in the peninsula, the religious significance of wells diminished, although many rural folk continued to regard them as places of healing and prophecy. As a result, people continued to visit these places and therefore many of the old well-traditions survived into the 19th century.

During the 18th century, as the Enlightenment blossomed, some people began to take a more rational view of the healing properties of wells, particularly those where the water had been scientifically analysed. A growing interest in antiquarianism and folklore, especially during the late 19th and early 20th centuries, resulted in a greater interest in all historic sites, including ancient holy wells.

In areas like Llŷn, despite the formidable opposition to well visits by the chapel authorities, many of the traditional beliefs and practices associated with wells, as well as age-old superstitions, persisted into the closing years of the 19th century. Even after the ancient well-culture had ceased to be observed, Llŷn wells continued to be important in people's lives until the middle years of the 20th century because they were still the only source of domestic water for inhabitants living in many small villages and isolated dwellings.

During the second half of the 20th century after the old well culture had faded from the scene and wells were no longer needed to supply water for daily use, many became neglected and lost. Today, however, there are signs of a rebirth of interest in the ancient wells of Wales, mainly on account of their connection with the pre-historic pagan tribes and the Celtic saints. We have seen how a few Llŷn wells have been granted 'Listed Building Status' and several others have been renovated in recent years. Moreover, there has been a resurgence of interest generally in the interesting folklore surrounding wells. However, we must not to be complacent in this matter.

Francis Jones has summed up the story of Welsh wells thus: 'Rooted in paganism, "converted" to Christian usage, condemned by Protestantism, "explained" by folklorists, rationalised by modern education, the cult has survived and still wields an influence over the human mind.' (Jones: *The Holy Wells of Wales*) Today such places are increasingly being viewed as important features of the historical landscape and noteworthy places on the 21st century tourist trail. Unfortunately many are continually at the mercy of aquatic weed, ferns, brambles and various other types of invading vegetation.

PART 11. AN INVENTORY OF THE ANCIENT WELLS OF THE LLŶN PENINSULA

Aberdaron – Ffynnon Saint

Ffynnon Saint is situated near the road which leads up the hill out of Aberdaron towards Uwchmymydd and Anelog. It is located in an area of dense scrub and woodland on the right hand side of the road opposite the National Trust Warden's house before the left turn to Uwchmynydd. Its position is marked by name on the O.S. Explorer Map No. 253.

In 1908 Myrddin Fardd recorded that this well was in a very poor state because many of its stones had been removed by workmen who were constructing a nearby bridge. In 2005 the AONB team also reported that it was so overgrown and in such a poor condition that they had difficulty finding it. In recent years access to the well has been improved by the Aberdaron Community Council. There is now a small slate roadside sign to indicate the well-site, and a narrow gravel path which leads to it between the trees.

The Royal Commission on Ancient and Historical Monuments in Wales (RCAHMW) records Ffynnon Saint as a 'holy well, possibly medieval in origin.' In plan it is a small D-shaped structure, measuring about 1 metre across, with stone walling below the water level. There is a stone wall, about 30cm. high, around it on three sides, and it is protected at ground level by a rectangular iron lid, hinged at the back. The water inside the well was very clear when the author inspected it.

Many years ago, when the water from this well was analysed by the medical sanitary inspector for Caernarfonshire, it was found to be of the purest quality. For many years the local people believed that Ffynnon Saint contained health-giving minerals. By mixing some of its water with white heather honey and gorse flowers, it is said that a local woman used to create a medicine which was considered particularly effective for the treatment of depression.

Aberdaron – Ffynnon Sarn y Felin

Ffynnon Sarn y Felin is situated on the right hand side of the B4413 when travelling down the hill into Aberdaron. As the road descends near the village the well can be seen on the right hand side. The water source is enclosed within a modern semi-circular stone structure, standing partly on the footpath and built against a recently-constructed stone wall which has a post and wire-mesh fence directly above it. The top of the semi-circular well-housing is fitted with an iron grille.

This well was discovered accidentally in 1999 during road widening works, and subsequently it was turned into a roadside feature with a wooden seat adjacent to it. Prior to its discovery nobody knew its original name or even of its existence. Consequently nothing is known about the well's history. Sarn y Felin (*sarn*: causeway; *y felin*: the mill) is a modern name, created by the people of Aberdaron in remembrance of the local village flour mill which closed over 50 years ago.

Abererch – Ffynnon Cawrdaf

Ffynnon Cawrdaf is located towards the bottom of a field belonging to Tanygraig Farm in Abererch parish, almost opposite the site of the Bryn Beryl Hospital. Therefore it is at the northern end of Abererch parish, a considerable distance from the parish church. Ffynnon Cawrdaf is described in RCAHMW as 'a well of unknown provenance', possibly a holy well and possibly post-medieval. At present this well, which is indicated by name on the 2.5 inches to 1mile O.S. Explorer Map No. 254, is protected by a small 19th century brick-built structure measuring 1.83 metres by 0.7 metres in plan. It is built into the side of a ridge which runs parallel to the Pwllheli-Caernarfon road.

The modern well-house, which faces the sea to the south-east, has a pitched roof, consisting of slates and clay ridge tiles, but it is in fairly poor condition. At one time the building was fitted with a wooden door although only the door frame now survives. When the author first saw it, the well house entrance was protected by a modern metal field gate which was secured across the doorway. The well building sits on top of stone slabs which may be ancient, according to RCAHMW. Inside the well house there is a rectangular basin. Myrddin Fardd recorded that Ffynnon Cawrdaf was reputed to be a healing well, which could cure any kind of ailment. It has been granted Grade II Listed status, although when the author viewed it for a second time it was found to be totally covered by invading vegetation.

The life story of Saint Cawrdaf is unclear. He is believed to have been born in about 495, the son of Caradog who was a tribal leader in the Brecon and Hereford area. He is reputed to have been a wise ruler and a charismatic warrior- leader and, according to one source, he was at one time 'one of the Three Chief Officers of Britain'. (David Nash Ford) Indeed, he may have been a person of considerable importance, for the 'Tale of the Dream of Rhonabwy' (the last of the 'Mabinogion' tales, probably written down during the 14th century but using material handed down from much earlier times by word of mouth) refers to him as a counsellor of King Arthur, the legendary Romano-Celtic leader. Eventually Cawrdaf is thought to have entered Saint Illtud's monastery in order to become a monk so that he could follow his religious calling. He is said to have founded and endowed several churches including the one at Abererch and another at Llangoed on Anglesey.

According to Baring-Gould and Fisher, a shrine once existed at Abererch, but it was not Saint Cawrdaf's shrine. *The Black Book of Carmarthen* states that Abererch was the burial place of

Rhydderch Hael, a Brythonic ruler from the 'Old North' of Britain, although other places are also reputed to be the site of his burial. Rhydderch is alleged to have achieved fame amongst the people of the Isle of Man after he defeated the Northumbrian King in battle during the late 6th century, thus saving the Manx people from invasion and subjection. Manx allegiance to Rhydderch was still in evidence as late as the 19th century, when it was recorded that Manx fishermen often interrupted their fishing in the Irish Sea so that they could sail into Pwllheli harbour and then visit Abererch Church on pilgrimage to pay homage to their hero.

During the Middle Ages the church at Abererch was probably one of the stopping places for pilgrims journeying to Enlli from the south. Baring-Gould and Fisher mention a megalith associated with Saint Cawrdaf at Abererch. They state, 'There is a Ffynnon Cawrdaf and, on a small eminence about a quarter of a mile from the church, is a large boulder stone, with a flat piece cut out of it, called Cadair Gawrdaf, his seat or chair.' Saint Cawrdaf is said to have been the brother of Saint Cadfarch who is also associated with a second well within Abererch parish.

Abererch – Ffynnon Gadfarch

According to Baring-Gould and Fisher, Cadfarch, the brother of Cawrdaf, was 'a saint or monk of Bangor Dunawd on the banks of the Dee near Wrexham and was formerly a patron of Abererch.' Bangor Dunawd is also known as Bangor Iscoed or Bangor-on-Dee. Baring-Gould and Fisher go on to state, 'There is a Ffynnon Gadfarch near the site of a now extinct capella, called Llangedwydd, at the northern end of Abererch parish'. In recent years, serious doubt has been cast upon the existence of a well chapel at this spot, and the statement by Baring-Gould and Fisher may have been written simply on the grounds that the prefix 'Llan' appears in the name Llangedwydd. Apparently the well was located south-east of Pont Rhyd Goch where the River Erch passes under the A499 Pwllheli to Caernarfon road. Today there is certainly no evidence of a well chapel at this point and there is nothing left of the well either, for the site has been modernised and the waters of the spring diverted into underground pipes.

At one time the water from Ffynnon Gadfarch was used regularly for baptisms in Abererch Parish Church, and on such occasions the baptismal water had to be carried all the way from the well to the church, a distance of approximately 2.5 miles as the crow flies. Obviously this well water was considered to be very special indeed! According to Francis Jones, during a baptism many years ago, water from a different source was used at a baptismal service instead of well water from Ffynnon Gadfarch. This caused the Abererch congregation to look on with 'considerable dread and misgivings' throughout the entire service.

Bodferin – Ffynnon Bibau or Ffynnon Trefgraig Bach

The old parish of Bodferin, situated inland from Porth Ferin and Porth Iago, is now part of the parish of Aberdaron. In 1843 Samuel Lewis wrote, 'The parish... on the shore of the Irish Sea... contains within its limits two small creeks called Porth Verin and Porth Iago, and there is a well called Ffynnon Bibau, near Trefgraig, which is the source of the river Daron.' Bryncroes-born Ieuan Lleyn, poet, eisteddfod competitor and schoolmaster also mentioned this well in 1799 during his 'Journey Through Lleyn': 'There's a house called Hendrefor and nearby a place called Trefgraig Plas, once an edifice of great dignity, close to where is Ffynnon Bibau and yet another river begins its journey to the sea here.' No record has been found to suggest that this well was either a holy well or a healing well. It was probably used as the domestic water supply for the nearby dwellings, although no further documentation could be found about its history.

Just over a mile to the west of Trefgraig is the ancient site of Saint Menin's Church, although nothing now remains of the building. This is probably the site of the church founded by a Celtic saint, variously known as Menin, Meirin or Merin who was the patron saint of the former parish of Bodferin. It is possible that, in the distant past, the well may have been a holy well, for there was perhaps an association between Saint Merin, the church that he founded and this well, although this is mere conjecture.

Bodferin – Ffynnon Saint

Ffynnon Saint, situated to the north-east of Anelog, was also mentioned in the letter written by Ieuan Lleyn in 1799. He wrote: 'Between Anelog and Carreg Plas there's a well, known as Ffynnon Saint (Holy Well) where the aforementioned river (Afon Saint) finds its source.' (Ieuan Lleyn: *A Jouney through Lleyn*) He also refers to a small chapel at Anelog where he saw early 6th century inscribed memorial stones, although they have since been moved for safe-keeping into Saint Hywyn's Church at Aberdaron. Those stones commemorate the burial of two priests, Veracius and Senacus along with their bretheren. It is thought that Capel Anelog was the site of a very early Christian community which existed before the monasteries were established on Ynys Enlli and at Aberdaron.

The community of monks probably established themselves here because there was a spring in the vicinity and therefore Ffynnon Saint may have been an important local holy well associated with that early Christian community.

Boduan – Ffynnon Buan

This well was mentioned in *Archaeologia Cambrensis* Vol. XIII 5th Series as being a well in the parish of Boduan. Since it bears the name of Saint Buan, a Celtic Saint who seems to have settled in this district, it must have been a holy well associated with this saint. According to Molly Miller (*The Saints of Gwynedd*) Saint Buan came to Gwynedd from the north of Britain. On Garn Boduan above Saint Buan's well are the remains of an extensive Iron Age stone fort with of many huts. The precise location of this well is not known and nothing further is known about its history.

Boduan – Ffynnon Wen

Another Boduan well, mentioned in Archaeologia Cambrensis Vol. XIII 5th Series, is Ffynnon Wen which is described as 'much thought of' and 'restored'. The author has not been able to locate this well and no additional information has been found about it.

Bodwrdda – Ffynnon Ddwrdan

In a remote spot on the bank of the river Daron, about a mile up stream from the village of Aberdaron, is Ffynnon Ddwrdan. It is situated to the north of the old house called Bodwrdda which, according to David Williams (*Dating Welsh Houses*: Bodwrdda) was first recorded in the 14th century. The well itself, which can be found beside the river where it flows through the middle of an area of pasture land, is simply a pool of water, covered by vegetation and surrounded by clumps of coarse marsh grass. The approach to it is extremely difficult. As David Williams states 'In the centre of the pastureland is an old spring, Ffynnon Ddwrdan. It is now a small artificial pond beside the river but even today you cannot see it from any public road, path or track and no building or other man made structure (apart from fencing) is visible from it!' The spring exhibits no evidence of masonry but it is probably an early medieval holy well originally associated with a Celtic saint called Dwrdan.

Very little is known about this saint although Rees (*Lives of the Cambro-British Saints*) states that he was one of the saints who followed Cadfan, the first abbot of Enlli, to Wales from Brittany. Sometimes recorded as Dirdan, he is mentioned in an ode to the first Tudor monarch, King Henry VII. His name is recorded in that poem amongst the names of more than one hundred other saints, to whose keeping the poet commits the king. (cited by Baring-Gould & Fisher) It is probable that Saint Dwrdan was a hermit who settled near this spring, and that is probably how the well (and subsequently the house – Bod + Dwrdan), acquired its name.

Ieuan Lleyn mentioned this well in 1799 after he had undertaken his 'Journey through Lleyn', 'Perhaps it (the house) should be Bodurdan as the well of Durdan isn't far.' In the distant past Ffynnon Ddwrdan may also have been the water supply for the nearby large medieval house.

Bryncroes – Ffynnon Cefn Leithfan

Ffynnon Cefn Lleithfan is situated on the eastern slope of Mynydd Rhiw. Myrddin Fardd stated that 'its shape is angular, about 2 yards wide and strongly walled around. Many came to it from near and far, especially those who were troubled by external cancers, for which its water is considered of great goodness...' By external cancers he meant warts. He also mentioned that, when approaching this well, it was essential for the patient to refrain from turning around or from speaking to anybody. Writing about Ffynnon Cefn Leithfan, and quoting from information provided by Myrddin Fardd, Sir John Rhŷs stated, 'What one has to do at the well is to bathe the warts with a rag or clout which has grease on it. When that is done, the clout with the grease has to be carefully concealed beneath the stone at the mouth of the well. This brings to my mind the fact that I have, more than once, years ago, noticed rags underneath stones in the water flowing from wells in Wales, and sometimes thrust into holes in the walls of wells, but I had no notion how they came there.'

The above narrative seems to suggest that such a ritual was far from unique to this particular well. If the correct procedure was followed, it was firmly believed that the warts would eventually disappear. Today this well has been modernised with a covering of concrete and an iron lid over it. There is a pipe attached through which water is seeping.

Bryncroes – Ffynnon Fair

Ffynnon Fair at Bryncroes is an ancient holy well with a rectangular basin, measuring 1.3 metres by 1.24 metres, aligned east to west. Inside the outer wall and extending around three sides are continuous stone steps (possibly of 17th century origin) which lead down to the pool. The enclosing wall is clearly much later. There is an entrance on one of the longer sides and a large stone has been let into the ground across the entrance to form a threshold. Water springs up into the well basin, forming a pool several inches deep. The outflow of water exits by means of a gulley at the base of the northern wall, from where it forms a fast flowing stream which travels down the hill before joining another stream at the lower end of a field.

This well, originally associated with Saint Mary's church, Bryncroes, is situated by the side of the road in the centre of the village, and a small chapel or capella called Tŷ Fair once stood nearby. In 1799 Ieuan Lleyn wrote, 'I make my way home past Bodgaua to the Church at Bryncroes, which is dedicated to the Virgin Mary, in Catholic times, close to the church are Ffynnon Fair, Tŷ Fair (Mary's house) Cae Fair (Mary's field).' (Ieuan Lleyn: 'A Journey Through Lleyn') Today there is no trace of Tŷ Fair, the small chapel.

Undoubtedly, in days gone by, this well was probably a healing well, judging from its stonework which was clearly designed for easy access to the water. No record of the conditions which its water was thought to cure has been found. It was also used for Christian baptism and indeed, according to the vicar of Bryncroes, water from the well is still used for that purpose in the parish church today. With a well chapel nearby Bryncroes was also probably a local place of pilgrimage.

The well and its surroundings are in excellent condition, the water is sparkling and it is evident that the entire site is extremely well looked after. Nevertheless, because it is in the centre of a village, this site tends to lack the special, tranquil atmosphere which pervades some of the more distant and remote well-sites.

Bryncroes – Ffynnon Lleuddad

Ffynnon Lleuddad is situated between Llangwnnadl and Sarn Meyllteyrn to the south-east of Carrog farmhouse at the northern end of the Bryncroes parish. According to the owners of Carrog, this well formerly existed in one of the fields belonging to the farm, together with a stream after which the farm is named. Writing in the first decade of the 20th century, Baring-Gould and Fisher stated, 'This was a walled well, of about four feet square, and was formerly in high repute for its cure of every manner of ailment in the case of both man and beast.' Ffynnon Lleuddad is marked by name on the O.S. Explorer Map no. 253 although very little evidence of it remains today. In 1964 RCAHMW described it as a spring partly surrounded by earthen banks. There is no suggestion that a chapel was ever associated with it.

The well was dedicated to Lleuddad or Laudatus who was an important Llŷn saint. According to Molly Miller (*The Saints of Gwynedd*) he was a north countryman. Together with Saint Cadfan he founded the monastery on Enlli (*Bardsey*), and it is believed that Lleuddad succeeded Cadfan as the monastery's second abbot. Saint Lleuddad's name is also remembered elsewhere in the area – Gerddi Lleuddad (the garden of Lleuddad) which is located opposite the chapel on Ynys Enlli while, on the coast near Aberdaron, is Ogof Lleuddad, a cave and hermitage where, according to tradition, Saint Lleuddad is said to have prayed from time to time.

There is a legend which tells how, when Abbot Lleuddad was on his death bed, an angel appeared to him. Lleuddad beseeched the angel to ensure that his monks on Enlli would live to a very great age, as long as they remained faithful servants. And so, according to tradition, it was the abbot's intercession which resulted in the monks living until they were very old. When Gerald of Wales visited Ynys Enlli in the 12th century he must have been aware of this legend for he wrote that the island 'from some miracle obtained by the merits of the saints, has this wonderful peculiarity, that the oldest people die first.'

Another legend relating to Saint Lleuddad, recorded in the 15th century by the poet Hywel ap Dafydd ap Ieuan ap Rhys, tells how the saint was milking a cow over a well on the island when all the water in the well suddenly turned to milk. A different version of the story records how the saint poured a bowlful of milk into the well and subsequently was able, by using his miraculous powers, to separate the milk from the water.

Carnguwch – Ffynnon Cae Garw

This well is situated in the northern part of Carnguwch on land belonging to Cae Garw farm. It is north-east of the farm on the right hand side of the road when travelling from Llithfaen towards Llanaelhaearn. It is marked on the O.S. Explorer map by the letter 'W'. Ffynnon Cae Garw is not known to be associated with any saint or church but it was reputed to be a healing well, particularly effective for the treatment of arthritis and warts. According to Myrddin Fardd, in order to get rid of warts, it was necessary to throw a different pin into the water for each individual wart.

The AONB team stated that the well was in an 'acceptable' condition when they visited it in 2005, but the water was 'streaming from the wall'. There is evidence of prehistoric settlement nearby, for on the top of Mynydd Carnguwch is a Bronze Age burial cairn, and there are also early hut groups in this area.

Carnguwch – Ffynnon Sanctaidd

Ffynnon Sanctaidd is located on the southern slope of Mynydd Carnguwch near Tyddyn Bach, and Francis Jones reported that, according to a document of 1893, water from this well was always kept in a container behind the door of the nearby church, together with a little brush. Each Sunday, as the members of the congregation entered the church for worship, they were sprinkled with water from the holy well, using the brush, which was referred to as *'ysgub y cwhwfan'* (the waving spirit) (cited by Francis Jones p. 82). When inspected in 2005 Ffynnon Sanctaidd was in a rather sad state, although clear water was flowing from it.

Clynnog Fawr – Ffynnon Beuno

Ffynnon Beuno, a Grade II listed monument, is one of the best surviving examples of a Llŷn holy well, and it is considered to be one of the most important wells on the peninsula. It is located on the left hand side of the original road (not the newly constructed road) between Clynnog Fawr and Llanaelhaearn. When travelling along the new road from Pwllheli look out for an illuminated Murco sign advertising the price of petrol at a garage. Adjacent to this sign is a right turn. Take this turn towards Clynnog village and after several yards at the T junction, turn right again onto the old road. A few yards along this road you will see the walled well on the left hand side. It is marked by name on the OS Explorer Map. Described by RCAHMW as 'a medieval holy well with later enhancements', Ffynnon Beuno is in excellent condition.

The well is situated about 4 metres back from the road and, to prevent misuse, the whole site is protected by a padlocked modern iron gate which is adjacent to the road. Beyond this gate there are several stone steps leading up to the well entrance which is protected by a second iron gate. The well itself is enclosed on all sides by a surrounding stone wall, measuring 4.0 metres long by 2.6 metres wide, and 2 metres in height. The top of this wall is finished with chamfered coping stones.

This structure is aligned on a north-east/south-west axis. Inside the surrounding wall is a rectangular stone basin measuring 1.6 metres by 2.0 metres. Around three sides of the basin there is a stone step which leads down to the pool. Above this step at the north-eastern and south-western sides are stone benches, above which are rectangular niches, two in the north-eastern wall and one on the south-western side. In the distant past, these small niches would probably have contained effigies of the saint. The entrance to the well is in the centre of the wall on the north-western side.

In medieval times this well would have been used by the monastic community at Clynnog Fawr as a source of water for domestic use and for religious rituals. Hughes and North (*The Churches of North Wales*) reported that the stonework of the well appeared to be of the same date as the church, which was rebuilt in the late 15th and early 16th centuries, although the coping stones are obviously much later, probably 18th century. People visiting Clynnog Fawr in the hope of securing a cure would visit both Saint Beuno's well and his chapel.

Saint Beuno's chapel, which is said to have been the burial place of Saint Beuno, is a separate 16th century building detached from the main body of the church. The original chapel and the 7th century monastery are said to have been destroyed by the Vikings in about 978. Excavations beside the church have revealed evidence of much earlier buildings and these may have been associated with Saint Beuno's original chapel.

In 1805, William Williams of Llandegai referred to the rebuilt chapel, as Eglwys y Bedd (*the church of the grave*). Writing of Saint Beuno's grave he stated, '... lately there was on the middle of the floor a stone piled as upon a grave and covered with a board on the top as with a flat stone.' (TCHS Vol. 39 1978) He goes on to report that, a few years previously, Lord Newborough had arranged for workmen to excavate Saint Beuno's grave inside the chapel but nothing was found. But Williams goes on to explain that those workmen were given lots of intoxicating liquor and that was probably the reason why they failed to dig down to a depth where they would be likely to find any human remains. The medieval monastery at Clynnog was dissolved at the time of the Protestant Reformation.

Until the 16th century Clynnog Fawr was an extremely important station and gathering point for pilgrims travelling the northern route to Ynys Enlli. Here, at the monastery, pilgrims would be able to rest and obtain food and drink. But Clynnog was also a place of pilgimmage in its own right, since it was the final resting place of Saint Beuno, the peninsula's most important saint. Because of its importance as a holy shrine, the monastery at Clynnog accumulated a great deal of wealth from the gifts of visiting pilgrims. A medieval chest, hewn from the trunk of an ash tree, with padlocks dating from about 1600, can still be seen inside the church. This is 'Cyff Beuno' into which pilgrims placed their gifts of money. When he was writing his *Survey of Caernarfonshire* in the early 19th century William Williams of Llandegai mentioned that offerings were still being made 'at the shrine of Saint Beuno at Clynnog and the other saints at their respective churches'. As a committed Protestant he deplored this practice.

On 15th April 1848 the Staffordshire Advertiser listed Ffynnon Beuno as one of three Welsh wells 'that everyone should visit and drink from.'

Saint Beuno, who is thought to have been born in Powys, travelled throughout the northern part of Wales although his cult is strongest in Llŷn where spent much of his life and where he was awarded the township of Clynnog by the King of Gwynedd. Here, at Clynnog early in the 7th century, he founded his monastery which became one of the most important religious centres in the kingdom. It was a 'clas' – a mother church where young people were trained and from where missionary monks went out into the surrounding area to spread the Christian gospel. It was a mixture of monastery and college. This religious establishment was considered to be so important that the Abbot of Clynnog was afforded a seat at the court of the King of Gwynedd. Beuno is the patron saint of the churches in Pistyll, Carnguwch, Deneio and Botwnnog as well as the church at Clynnog..

According to popular legend, Saint Beuno possessed miraculous healing powers, for he is alleged to have carried out several miracles. He is said to have restored back to life his disciple, Saint Aelhaearn (who had been torn to pieces by wild animals), his own niece, Saint Winifred (who had been decapitated by a rejected suitor) and Princess Digwig (whose head had been cut off by the young man whom she had recently married). See the sections about Ffynnon Aelhaearn and Ffynnon Ddigwig for these stories about Saint Beuno's miraculous powers.

In the tradition of Saint Beuno, the water from this well was believed to possess wonderful curative properties, and there is written evidence which confirms that, as late as the 18th century, this well was being used for healing a variety of complaints, including epilepsy and paralysis. Those who were incapable of walking were carried to the well so that they could be lowered bodily into the well water. Having bathed at the well, infirm patients often spent the night sleeping on top the saint's flat tomb in Saint Beuno's chapel.

After Thomas Pennant (*A Tour in Wales*) had visited Clynnog Church in the 1770s he wrote, 'Votaries were wont to have great faith in him (Saint Beuno) and did not doubt but that by means of a night's lodging on his tomb a cure would be found for all diseases. It was customary to cover it with rushes and leave on it till morning sick children, after making them first undergo ablution in the neighbouring Holy Well; and I myself once saw on top of it a feather bed, on which a poor paralytic from Merioneddshire had lain the whole night after undergoing the same ceremony.'

There was also a popular belief that water from Saint Beuno's Well, mixed with stone dust, scraped from the columns of the pillars in Clynnog church, created an excellent lotion for soothing tired eyes. Hughes and North suggest that the scrapings were probably taken from the medieval pillars in Saint Beuno's chapel. Such healing rituals are evidence of the tremendous faith which the people of Wales had in this saint's powers!

Clynnog Fawr – Ffynnon Nantcall

This well in Clynnog Fawr parish is mentioned by Myrddin Fardd and by Francis Jones, and it is also recorded on a database of historic monuments in North Wales. Unfortunately the author has not been able to locate it. Several illnesses, including melancholy and indigestion, were said to be cured by its water.

Cricieth – Ffynnon Saint

Like the old parish church in Cricieth, Ffynnon Saint was dedicated to Saint Catherine and therefore it must have been a holy well, although originally it was probably dedicated to a local Celtic saint. The dedication to Saint Catherine, a Middle Eastern martyr, probably dates from the late 13th/early 14th century by which time her cult had spread to the west.

This well was situated near to Ger y Maes, the end house on Holywell Terrace, which is located at the upper end of the Y Maes (*the Green*). It was formerly a holy well and a healing well, as suggested by the name of the adjacent terrace of houses. Tradition suggests that Ffynnon Saint was visited on Easter Sundays when pins and keys were thrown into the water to give solace to the patron saint and to seek her blessing. As a healing well it was considered to be especially good for curing eye infections.

Ffynnon Saint was also formerly an important source of domestic water for the town's people of Cricieth. The site was partly cut out of the rock and there was also some man-made stonework associated with it, including a set of steps leading down to a sunken basin. When the well was inspected in the late 1950s it was said to be "encumbered with garage scrap." Unfortunately this well no longer exists, for it was destroyed in the 1960s to make way for building work on the site. What a pity that this ancient monument had to be destroyed!

This well is mentioned in a paper written in 1809. It states that 'in former times no one liked to have his child baptised except with (or in) water from Ffynnon-y-Saint which was brought over Bryn yr Eglwys, over the old path which I hear is allowed to be closed, as also the old well, being inadmissible.' This information was quoted in the *North Wales Chronicle* dated 11th August 1877 in an article about Old Cricieth.

There was also a natural well inside the house at Ger y Maes. Eira and James Gleasure (*Cricieth: A Heritage Walk*) state that, many years ago, the spring water from this internal well was used by the occupants of the house in the production of ginger beer. The ginger beer was bottled in old-fashioned cod bottles with marble stoppers in their necks and then sold directly to customers who called at this house to purchase it.

Cricieth – Pistyll Bach

Situated beside the Caernarfon Road, a little further up the hill from the 'Roman Catholic Church of The Holy Spirit' and on the same side of the road as that church, is the site of a former spring called Pistyll Bach. (*Cricieth: A Heritage Walk*) It is sunk into the wall although the outlet is now blocked so that no water emerges at ground level. Presumably, having left this spot, the water from the spring flowed in an underground gully to join the Afon Cwrt, the small river which flows down the hill through Y Maes. Nothing further is known about the history of this well.

Glasfryn – Ffynnon Grasi

A Llŷn well which is mentioned at some length by Sir John Rhŷs in his chapter on the 'Folklore of the Wells' is Ffynnon Grasi or Grace's Well, which he describes as a 'fairy well'. Originally it was perhaps a holy well and it may be medieval in origin. It is to be found at Glasfryn Uchaf, at the north eastern end of the Glasfryn Lake. It is situated to the east of the larger of the two standing stones and beneath a field bank at the head of the lake. In 1960 RCAHMW described it as 'approximately an oval basin 14ft long by 10 ft wide, surrounded by an irregular drystone wall 1ft 6ins to 3ft thick and up to 2 ft high above the external ground level. At the western side, facing the lake, two rough stone steps lead up to the lowest point of the wall.' At present the whole structure is in a dilapidated state, for it consists simply of a fairly large pool with only traces of the surrounding stonework, much of which has disappeared. The entire site is now surrounded by a wire fence and clumps of trees.

At one time this well was a source of domestic water for the nearby houses. According to local tradition the well used to be protected by a cover, which was supposed to be kept closed unless water was being drawn. A legend, which was still commonly believed at the end of the 19th century, tells how a young girl called Grasi, having obtained water, accidentally forgot to replace the well cover, thus causing the water to overflow to such an extent that Glasfryn lake was formed. Grasi became so distraught by what she had done that for ever afterwards she wandered up and down the higher ground, in the field called Cae'r Ladi, howling and weeping.

Another version of the story alleges that when Grasi allowed the waters to escape to form the lake, fairies seized her and turned her into a swan as a punishment, an earthly form which she kept for many years until she eventually died. Ever since her death, so the story goes, her ghost has continued to moan and shriek alarmingly at the dead of night, as she bemoans her misfortune. In the past, according to Sir John Rhŷs, many local people claimed to have heard her shrill cries, especially at 2 o'clock in the morning, and one or two locals maintained that they had actually seen her. Such stories are not unique in Wales for several other Welsh wells are associated with tales of ghosts.

There were rumours, too, that Grasi haunted the nearby house of the Williams-Ellis family at Glasfryn. Sir John Rhŷs recorded how he and his wife once had the pleasure of staying at Glasfryn with Mrs. Williams-Ellis, but he was at pains to point out that their sleep was never disturbed by Grasi's wailing at any time during their stay.

According to another legend, one of the pair of standing stones which is situated nearer to the well is the figure of Grasi, turned to stone as a puishment for her negligence. Those two standing stones near the well are thought to date from the Early Bronze Age and therefore it is possible that there may have been some sort of pagan religious association between the well and the stones.

Llanaelhaearn –Ffynnon Aelhaearn

Having left the main Caernarfon-Pwllheli road, (A499) you will be able to see Ffynnon Aelhaearn on the B4417 road to Nefyn. As you approach the top of the hill, when travelling towards Nefyn, the well is situated on the left hand side of the road, by the side of a house called Bryn Iddon and almost opposite the 'Llanaelhaearn' village sign. This well is enclosed within one of the largest stone-built well structures on the peninsula.

Ffynnon Aelhaearn is unusual in that the well is completely enclosed within a low, roofed building, the front elevation of which is topped with blocks of stone in a pattern resembling the crenellations on a castle wall. Behind this facade there is a flat roof which slopes down from front to back. The entrance faces the road and has a boarded door, above which a small slate plaque reads 'Saint Aelhaiarn's Well Roofed 1900'. The external dimensions of the wellhouse are 5.95m by 5.59m. Internally, there is a walkway and a continuous stone seat surrounding the water basin which measures 3.96m by 2.14m. RCAHMW stated in 1960 that 'the basin and surrounding stone bench are probably medieval.'

Unfortunately, the door to this well-building is kept padlocked and therefore access to the interior is prohibited. When the AONB team first visited this well they stated that the interior of the building was in a state of disrepair and the 'roof and door were in poor condition.' Since their initial visit Ffynnon Aelhaearn has been completely refurbished, the well chamber having been cleaned out and a new roof and door fitted. This work was completed in 2005.

There is clear evidence of early Christian settlement at Llanaelhaearn in the form of inscribed stones at Saint Aelhaearn's church. One of those stones is a 5th or early 6th century memorial to a person called Aliotus, who was a native of the independent kingdom of Elmet (now part of Yorkshire). Aliotus may have fled to North Wales when Elmet was attacked by the Saxons. This stone was found in a small ancient enclosure of church land which lay beyond the churchyard, suggesting that it was connected to the early Celtic Church here. (*TCHS* No. 47 1986) There is also a second inscribed stone originating from the same period. A third one dating from 5th to 7th century can be seen in the churchyard wall although it is not known where this stone was originally sited.

Both the well and the church at Llanaelhaearn are dedicated to Saint Aelhaearn, who is believed to have been a follower of Saint Beuno. Like his mentor, Saint Aelhaearn came originally from Powys and indeed he may have accompanied Saint Beuno northwards to Gwynedd. Like Saint Beuno's well at Clynnog Fawr, Ffynnon Aelhaearn was an important holy well during the Middle Ages. It was also a pilgrim well, and there is no doubt that the presence of this bountiful spring was the determining factor in the establishment of a settlement at this precise spot.

We know that this area was inhabited in pre-Christian times. Ffynnon Aelhaearn lies in the shadow of the Tre'r Ceiri Iron Age fort and a little to the north, on lower ground, is the site of an enclosed homestead which is probably of Romano-Brythonic origin. This enclosed settlement may have been associated with the fort above it (*TCHS* No. 47 1986). Therefore it may be assumed that there was probably a connection in pre-Christian times between the well and the tribespeople who lived in this area.

The name 'Aelhaearn' means 'iron brow'. Baring-Gould and Fisher recount a legend which purports to explain how Saint Aelhaearn acquired his name. It states that one day, as he journeyed around the countryside, Aelhaearn was attacked by fierce wild animals which tore him to pieces. Fortunately Saint Beuno came that way, so he gathered up all the body parts and reassembled them. Since a small piece of bone above the eye was missing Saint Beuno improvised by repairing the damage, by using a piece of iron from the end of a spear – hence the name 'iron brow'. After re-assembling his colleague Saint Beuno restored him back to life by using his miraculous, life-giving powers. Pennant mentions this legend in passing but he does not dwell upon it, simply describing the story as 'too absurd to relate.'

Originally Ffynnon Aelhaearn was roofless and therefore open to the elements for, like many other Llŷn wells, it was simply surrounded by a stone wall just a few feet high. During the Middle Ages Ffynnon Aelhaearn was almost certainly an important resting point on the northern pilgrim route to Enlli. Having struggled up the steep hill towards the well and site of Llanaelhaearn church, pilgrims must have welcomed the opportunity to pause and rest, seek Saint Aelhaearn's blessing, drink some cool refreshing water from his well, bathe their aching feet and make use of the well's curative powers to treat any medical conditions from which they were suffering.

Eventually, when Llŷn religious pilgrimages had ceased, the importance of Ffynnon Aelhaearn as a holy well diminished, and this is confirmed by Pennant's comment, 'Near is a fine well, once much frequented because of its sanctity.' This statement confirms that, by the 1770s, the well was no longer visited for religious purposes. This was due largely to the decline of Catholicism in these parts and the subsequent rapid growth of Nonconformity after the Reformation. Ffynnon Aelhaearn was not mentioned at all by William Williams of Llandegai when he was writing his survey of Caernarfonshire in 1806.

Nevertheless, for many years during the 19th century, this well continued to be recognised by people as an effective healing well. Baring-Gould and Fisher describe the procedure which people adopted at this well when seeking a cure: '... there are seats of stone ranged along the sides for the accommodation of the "troubling of the waters". The troubling of the waters is a singular phenomenon. At regular intervals, and at various points in the basin, the crystal water suddenly wells up, full of sparkling bubbles. Then ensues a lull and again a swell of water occurs in another part of the tank... Locally it was called the laughing of the water.' As soon as bubbles started to rise to the surface it was a sign that it was the best time for the patient to descend the steps to bathe. This bubbling effect in the water is mentioned in connection with several other Welsh wells.

Long after Ffynnon Aelhaearn had ceased to be used for religious and healing purposes it continued to provide drinking water for the inhabitants of the village. In 1900 the height of the external surrounding wall was raised by the Parish Council and a flat concrete roof (which slopes down from front to rear) was added, thus completely enclosing the well basin. This work was carried out in order to safeguard the village's water supply after several cases of diptheria had appeared in the village. Writing in 1924, Hughes and North stated that they were not impressed by the addition of this roof. They commented, 'For less money something appropriate and beautiful could have been provided.' But they did comment that 'there was a great flow of water' from the well.

After Ffynnon Aelhaearn had been taken over by the local water board it continued to provide the nearby dwellings with their water supply until the mid 20th century when the Cwm Ystradllyn water scheme was constructed to bring a piped water supply the whole of Llŷn. Today there is some confusion over the ownership of the well and that is probably the reason why the door is kept padlocked.

After leaving Ffynnon Aelhaearn the water flows in an underground culvert towards the river. In the 19th century this outflow ran in an open gulley beneath the buildings at Tyddyn y Llan where there was a small mill for grinding gorse into horse feed. It was the water flowing away from Ffynnon Aelhaearn which powered this mill. In 1893, the 57 year old local vicar, The Revd Hugh Edward Williams, was tragically killed when he was dragged into the mill's machinery as he tried to free a blockage in the system, using a pitchfork. His memorial tablet can be seen on the wall inside Llanaelhaearn church.

Llanbedrog – Ffynnon Bedrog

Situated 200 ft. above sea level in a field at Bryn Ddu, this well is marked by name on the O.S. Explorer Map 253. In 1960 it was described by RCAHMW as a small well with a rubble-walled rectangular basin 3ft (0.9m) by 1ft 6ins (0.45m) and known locally as 'The Wishing Well'. In 1960 it was reported to be in good condition although covered with boulders. It is said that in recent years it has been virtually obliterated by vegetation, for a Snowdon Heritage Information Sheet states that 'the area of the well is now overgrown and it is not known exactly where it is.' Certainly the author was unable to locate this well. He walked the entire path across Bryn Ddu but the land on either side was badly overgrown with bracken and bramble. He enquired of the well's whereabouts at a nearby house but the occupant said that she did not know of its precise position, simply waving her hand vaguely in the direction of Bryn Ddu and saying, 'It is somewhere over there, I believe'. She added that there was little chance of finding it since everywhere was so badly overgrown.

Originally Ffynnon Bedrog was a holy well of considerable importance. Baring–Gould and Fisher wrote of it, 'It enjoyed a great reputation formerly, and many traditions linger of the miraculous cures effected by its waters, in every conceivable ailment ... In the 16th and 17th centuries it was there considered to be beneficial to offer to Pedrog for gangrenes.' Gangrene is a life-threatening medical condition in which body tissue starts to decompose due to lack of circulation or serious infection. The treatment of gangrene at Ffynnon Bedrog involved bathing the affected body part in the well water.

Ffynnon Bedrog was also used for detecting thieves. To discover the truth about a theft the aggrieved person would throw pieces of bread into the pool one at a time whilst at the same time calling out the names of the suspects. If a piece of bread floated as a name was spoken that person was innocent but if the bread sank the guilty party had been found. This practice is similar to the medieval practice of trial by water, the only difference being that in the Middle Ages it was the suspected thief himself or herself who was thrown into an area of water to sink or float.

Long ago Ffynnon Bedrog was a well where gifts of pins were offered, for Myrddin Fardd recorded in 1908 that a round vessel made of black stone, which had recently been found at the bottom of the well, was full of pins.

As its name suggests Ffynnoon Bedrog is dedicated to Saint

Pedrog, a 6th century Celtic saint who is believed to have been the son of a king, probably from Cornwall. It is said that Pedrog gave up the chance to inherit his father's kingdom in order to become a monk. He is thought to have spent a great deal of his time in Cornwall where he is known as Saint Petroc and where he established monasteries at both Padstow and Bodmin. Many churches in Devon and Cornwall are dedicated to him. He is the patron saint of three churches in Wales – the church here at Llanbedrog, another in Pembrokeshire where he is known as Saint Petrox (an alternative spelling of his name) and a third near Cardigan.

We cannot be certain if Saint Pedrog ever visited this part of Wales. According to accounts of his life he travelled extensively to Brittany, Rome, Jerusalem and India and therefore it is possible that he may also have visited the monastery on Ynys Enlli as many of the early saints did. It is thought that Pedrog died in Cornwall in about 564 and was buried in Padstow although later his relics were transferred to Bodmin when the Padstow priory was ransacked by the Vikings. Subsequently his bones were returned to Saint Petroc's church, Bodmin where to this day they are kept in an ivory casket.

Llanbedrog – Ffynnon Trwy'r Nant

At the bottom of the hill on the road (B4413 Ffordd Pedrog) which runs through the village and opposite the gates to the school there is a lane called Trwy'r Nant. Towards the end of that lane on the left hand side there is a rough track which leads to a footpath with a green-painted metal gate. Beyond the green gate on the left hand side of the footpath is Ffynnon Trwy'r Nant. This well is marked with a letter 'W' on the O.S. Explorer Map No. 253 but it is not named.

The rectangular well site measures approximately 4.5 metres by 1.5 metres and it consists of a deep sunken area enclosed by green-painted railings. The site looks very tidy and the railings have been repainted recently. There is an open entrance in the railings, leading to several steps which descend to the water source which seems to be fed by a stream flowing down the hill past the site and into the valley. Little is known about the history of this well but since the steps and the sunken area are constructed of concrete they are undoubedly fairly modern. It is possible that Ffynnon Trwy'r Nant was formerly the main source of domestic water for the inhabitants of Llanbedrog for it is very close to the main street and therefore would have been easily accessible to the inhabitants of the village.

Llandudwen – Ffynnon Dudwen

This ancient well near Dinas, about two miles to the east of Tudweiliog, is situated in a quiet, isolated spot in a corner of a field. It is a rather remote spot for there is no village now, just a secluded church and a farm. To find the well, proceed towards Madryn Castle from the village of Dinas, and after about three-quarters of a mile you will see a narrow lane on your left. Proceed down this lane towards Tan Llan Farm and Llandudwen Church where you will find several parking spaces. The original Saint Tudwen's church is reputed to have been built on the site of Saint Tudwen's grave.

The well can be reached by walking back up the lane until you see a kissing gate on your left. Go through the kissing gate and head diagonally to the left across the field (which may be slightly boggy in parts) towards another kissing gate. Walk across this second field towards a wooden stile which leads to the well-site. From the other side of this stile, the well itself can be seen to the right, where it is marked by a large wooden cross.

Ffynnon Dudwen is associated with a hermit called Saint Tudwen, who is alleged have been one of the daughters of a local Welsh king. It is said that she established her cell here, thus giving her name to both the well and the church. She is reputed to have had extraordinary healing powers, as did her well. Just over half a mile to the east lies the Iron Age site at Wyddgrug and one mile to the south is the hill fort at Garn Fadrun.

According to Myrddin Fardd the water from Ffynnon Dudwen was effective for treating several ailments including eye infections, rheumatism, weakness of the tendons, numbness, epilepsy and fainting fits. He states that people used to travel considerable distances to seek treatment at this well. Having arrived here, they would throw coins and new pins into the water in the expectation of being healed. It has been said that local farmers also came to the well in the hope that Saint Tudwen would bless them and increase their crop yields. Myrddin Fardd also records that this site was a place where baptisms and clandestine marriages were conducted.

Ffynnon Dudwen, which was clearly not on the pilgrim route, never achieved the notoriety of certain other Llŷn wells like Ffynnon Beuno and Ffynnon Aelhaearn, and so, after a time, it became neglected, probably owing to the remoteness and inaccessability of the site, Myrddin Fardd suggests.

Ffynnon Dudwen, which is a natural spring, is situated at the base of a grassy bank, beneath a roughly-constructed, semi-circular wall of substantial boulders. This wall, which varies between about 0.61m to 0.92m tall, retains the earth bank behind it as it sweeps around the pool in an arc, decreasing in height as it approaches the front. There are no neatly-constructed walls enclosing the well pool, and there are no stone seats, walkways or niches such as those which can be seen at certain other Llŷn holy wells. The RCAHMW described Ffynnon Dudwen simply as 'Remains of a basin (originally the spring) 6 ft diameter and 3 ft from front to back. Associated with St Tudwen's church.' Earlier written records provide a similar description – a stone wall about 3 feet (0.92m) high at the back, which gradually becomes lower as it sweeps around the sides. At the front there is a threshold of smooth stones to retain the water.

When Myrddin Fardd was writing in 1908 he stated that the well was in a very poor condition. He wrote, 'Now nothing is left of the old well, no more than a spot on the edge of a field near the church – time has broken it up and buried it in its own pool.' In 1907 Baring-Gould and Fisher confirmed that the well had disappeared completely. Nearly one hundred years later, in his book *Llŷn*, Elfed Gruffydd described Ffynnon Dudwen as 'completely overgrown'. Apparently the undergrowth was so dense that it was almost impossible to see the water.

However in recent years, with the land owner's permission and funded by Gwynedd County Council, a team of AONB workmen under the direction of Bleddyn Prys Jones cleared the site of vegetation to reveal the semicircular well. The stone wall at the rear of the well has now been exposed so that, once again, its dimensions can be seen as described by the RCAHMW.

Following this renovation work, a fence was erected around the well-site to prevent livestock from trampling through it. Traditional kissing gates, made by a local craftsman, were installed to provide access across the fields, so that once again people may visit this tranquil spot as they used to do hundreds of years ago. In the spring of 2011 Ffynnon Dudwen was re-consecrated by the Bishop of Bangor.

Llanengan – Ffynnon Engan

Ffynnon Engan is situated a short distance from Llanengan church, to the north- west of the graveyard, on land at the side and rear of a row of cottages. It is an ancient holy well associated with Saint Einion (also known as Saint Engan) to whom, in addition to the well, the church at Llanengan is dedicated. This well is not mentioned at all by Francis Jones in *The Holy Wells of Wales*.

Einion, who is believed to have been a descendent of Cunedda, was Prince of Llŷn and a patron of the early Christian Church in the peninsula. It is believed that he also had some jurisdiction in Anglesey where it is said that he granted Seiriol land so that he could establish the priory at Penmon and a hermitage on Puffin Island. According to some sources Einion also persuaded Cadfan to come from Tywyn to Llŷn where he is said to have given him the Isle of Enlli. Here they jointly established the great monastery so that it could 'become a monastic refuge for Saints who were weary of the world'. Einion is also said to have founded the first church at Llanengan and later on he is alleged to have joined Cadfan's community on Enlli. It was these activities which resulted in Prince Einion being regarded as a special saint.

According to tradition Saint Einion was buried in Llanangan church and his tomb and shrine became a significant place of pilgrimage. When pilgrims flocked here, they placed their gifts of money into the cyff or chest inside the church. The medieval 'Cyff Engan', hollowed out of a single baulk of timber and protected by iron bands and three heavy iron locks, can still be seen inside the church which was rebuilt around 1520.

The well itself is situated at the foot of a bank, with stone retaining walls on the northern and eastern sides to prevent the soil from collapsing into the pool. There is a water-filled, walled basin 3 metres square and half a metre deep. Two continuous stone steps run around the pool on the northern, eastern and southern sides. The spring enters at the south-eastern corner and the outlet is on the western side. From here the water runs in a gully down the slope towards a stream in the valley. There is evidence of an Iron Age hill fort about 350 yards to the south of Llanengan.

The well of Engan was believed to possess special healing properties, and centuries ago large numbers of children and adults, journeying here on pilgrimage, would bathe themselves in the waters of this spring, convinced of its healing properties. The well was still considered important during the 15th century because, in his poem about King Einion, Hywel ap Dafydd ap Ieuan ap Rhys ('Hywel Dafi' the 15th century Welsh poet) makes reference to the well of Engan being strengthened. Pilgrimages to Llanengan were taking place in the 1530s for, when he undertook his tour of Wales in 1536-9 Leland remarked that there 'was late a great Pilgrimage here'. It is not known when exactly people ceased to visit this well for the purposes of healing. In 1907 Baring-Gould and Fisher reported that water from this well was being used in the church for baptisms. Ffynnon Engan is a Grade II listed monument and, having been cleared and restored recently, the author found it to be in excellent condition when he visited it on two occasions.

Llanengan – Ffynnon Tudwal

Writing about Ffynnon Tudwal, Myrddin Fardd states that this well 'on the land of Penrhyn in Llanengan parish... cured wounds and various illnesses.' Baring-Gould and Fisher also state that this well 'formerly existed on Penrhyn in the parish of Llanengan.' When they wrote Penrhyn they meant the headland at Penrhyn Du which overlooks Abersoch and Saint Tudwal's Islands. Baring and Fisher described the well as 'a beautiful spring of crystal water, which has now been drained dry by the local lead mine.'

There was a record of lead-mining activity on Penrhyn Du in the 17th, 18th and 19th centuries, and there is clear documentary evidence that, during this period, there were considerable drainage problems at the Penrhyn Du lead mines. It is probable that Ffynnon Tudwal was destroyed in an attempt to safeguard the mining activity.

Who was Saint Tudwal, and did this well have any religious significance? In his TCHS article (Vol.21 1960) about the church on Saint Tudwal's Island Douglas B Hague wrote, 'All that can be said with any confidence of Saint Tudwal is that he was a Briton who emigrated to Brittany in the 6th century. He was consecrated bishop and ended his days in the monastery he had founded at Treher... His association, if any, with these islands is lost in the mists of time.'

There was a priory on Saint Tudwal's East during the Middle Ages, for it is mentioned in the Norwich Valuation of 1245 although we do not know when it was first established. The priory is mentioned again in a taxation document of 1291 as *Ecclesia Prioris de Enys Tudwal*. It was still functioning in 1410 for, during that year, the abbot is recorded as Ieuan ap Blethin. *Arch. Camb.* 1922) Then came the Reformation and, by Leland's time in the 16th century, its church was described as 'desolate'.

Some sources suggest that Saint Tudwal was of royal birth, the son of King Hoel I (The Great) who was exiled from Brittany to Britain. After having travelled to Ireland to learn the scriptures, Tudwal is thought to have returned to Wales to become a hermit on Saint Tudwal's Island, where the priory was later established. Ffynnon Tudwal, is probably dedicated to Saint Tudwal because of his association with the area and its offshore island. Later on, as Douglas B. Hague stated, Tudwal appears to have emigrated from Wales to Brittany where he travelled around the countryside evangelising the population. He is also said to have founded two Breton monasteries, including the one at Tréguire (Treher) where he was subsequently appointed bishop and where he died in 564 Saint Tudwal is the patron saint of several Breton towns.

Llanfaelrhys – Ffynnon Nant-y-Gadwen

This natural spring is situated on a slope due south of the village of Llanfaelrhys, above the valley called Nant y Gadwen and beneath the manganese mine workings of the same name. The well is also sometimes referred to as Ffynnon Maelrhys. It is said that Breton-born Saint Maelrhys, who also gave his name to the nearby village, came to Llŷn with Saint Cadfan. He is revered on the holy island of Enlli but very little is known about his life and work. The church at Llanfaelrhys is the only church dedicated to this saint. No more information could be found about the well's history but the nearby mine, which was opened in the early 19th century, was one of the most important manganese mines in Britain until it closed in 1927.

Llangybi – Ffynnon Llety Plu

Today Ffynnon Llety Plu is no more than a depression in the ground filled with muddy water and therefore it is scarcely worth viewing. To reach it follow the brown road signs which direct you to Ffynnon Gybi. Eventually a brown sign instructs you to leave the road and follow a footpath along a wide track. Ffynnon Llety Plu is on the left hand side of this track as you walk towards Ffynnon Gybi. The well is marked on the O.S. Explorer Map map 254 by the letters 'Spr'. Originally Ffynnon Llety Plu was named after a nearby property (Llety Plu), now a private dwelling but formerly an inn or public lodging house, for its Welsh name translated into English means 'The Feathers Inn'. Ffynnon Llety Plu was almost certainly the domestic water supply for the inn as well as for the other nearby cottages, the ruined remains of which can be seen further along the track.

Llangybi – Ffynnon Gybi

Ffynnon Gybi, which is the only Llŷn well-site to have been granted Grade I Listed Status, is the most elaborate and most interesting one on the peninsula. Now in the care of CADW, this well-site is situated in a tranquil valley behind the church of Saint Cybi beneath the hill of Garn Bentyrch on which there are the remains of Iron Age fortifications. Because of its proximity to those ancient forts Ffynnon Gybi may have been used by the Iron Age peoples in their pagan religious rituals, although there is no hard evidence to support this. This well itself is dedicated to Saint Cybi, one of the important 6th century saints of North Wales.

Saint Cybi appears to have come from Cornwall, where he was probably of noble birth. According to tradition, he is thought to have travelled to Jerusalem, Rome and France where he received his religious training. After a period of time spent in Ireland he sailed from Wicklow to Llŷn. Having landed on the peninsula, he walked inland to the place now known as Llangybi. Later on, he moved to the old Roman fort at Holyhead on Anglesey where he established a religious community. There is a legend which tells that, after Saint Cybi had moved to Holyhead he used to meet up regularly with Saint Seriol who had established himself at Penmon on the eastern side of the island. It is said that the two saints regularly met up in the centre of the island. On such occasions Saint Gybi walked facing the sun in the morning and returned to Holyhead facing the setting sun in the evening. He became known as Cybi Felyn or Cybi the Golden, because his face was tanned by the sun. On the other hand Saint Seriol became known as Seriol Wyn or Seriol the Pale because he always walked with his back to the sun. Francis Jones has identified five Welsh wells dedicated to Saint Cybi – two on the Isle of Anglesey, one in the former county of Cardiganshire, one in Monmouthshire and this one in Gwynedd.

Writing in *Archaeologia Cambrensis* in 1904 William Williams stated that Saint Cybi first established his base at Llangybi and that Maelgwyn, King of Gwynedd, 'made acquaintance with him here'. It was Maelgwyn, he suggests, who granted Cybi his land in Angelsey where the saint subsequently founded his monastery. *Arch. Camb.* 1904 Vol. IV Series 6 According to legend, when he arrived in Llangybi the saint plunged his staff into the ground, causing a spring of water, now known as Ffynnon Gybi, to flow from the spot. This seems to be a recurring theme in the lives of the saints because several other Welsh holy wells are reputed to have been formed after saints had struck the ground with their staffs e.g. Saint Gwynllyw's Well (Glamorgan) and Saint Illtud's Well (Gower).

Saint Cybi's well used to be a noted place for pilgrimage and, like so many of the Llŷn wells, it was both a holy well and an extremely effective place of healing. For this reason it continued to be popular long after the Reformation and, according to CADW 'there was still a box for offerings, Cyff Gybi, in the church during the 18th century.' We cannot be sure when the tradition of going on pilgrimage to Ffynnon Gybi started but the site must have been considered a holy one during the Middle Ages.

The well can be reached in one of two ways. Either you can follow the brown signs which direct you along the roads until finally you are instructed to go down a wide rough track – the same track that was mentioned in the previous section about Ffynnon Llety Plu. This route eventually leads to a primitive stone bridge across a stream and onto a stone causeway which traverses the Ffynnon Gybi site. Long ago this would have been the main means of access to the well-site. Alternatively you can climb over a stile at the eastern end of the churchyard, follow the path to the bottom of the field, cross another stile, and continue down the side of that field into the valley until you come to the Ffynnon Gybi site.

Ffynnon Gybi has two well buildings, both of which are built of large blocks of stone. The larger building, which contains the principal well basin, is formed of dry unmortared walling, a metre thick in places, and there are traces of a vaulted roof with corbelling, reminiscent of early Irish cells. This building measures approximately 5 metres square and is about 3.5 metres high with a door in the south wall. Inside this building there is a sunken pool surrounded by a paved walkway from which steps lead down to the pool. Built into the thickness of the interior walls are several recesses which once served as seats.

There is some confusion about the date of this well chamber. Lord Harlech suggested that it may date from the early Christian period. (*Illustrated Regional Guides to North Wales* Vol. V) If that suggestion is correct then this well chamber would be one of the oldest surviving Christian buildings in Wales. Both Frances Lynch (In her book *Gwynedd*) and Francis Jones also state that the main well chamber is probably early. CADW is more cautious, stating that this building is of indeterminate date. RCAHMW, on the other hand, maintains that all the buildings on the Llangybi site probably date from the mid 18th century and that the ancient appearance of the well chamber may be 'due to conscious archaism of the 18th century squire' who owned the site and who developed it as a healing spa. However, if RCAHMW's assertion is correct, the 18th century owner must have gone to considerable lengths to ensure that this building looked convincingly like an early medieval structure!

Attached to the rear of the main well chamber is a second smaller well building, inside which the spring rises to form a small pool. Like the main building this well-chamber also has a ledge and steps. From this small pool the water feeds forwards into the principal basin within the larger well house. The outlet is at the front of this main building, where a stream emerges into a stone-lined channel before flowing across the field towards the stream.

Adjoining the main well-chamber is an 18th century cottage, with its entrance in the south wall. The cottage has much thinner walls and they are constructed of mortared masonry. Many years ago this cottage, which was the residence of the well keeper, also provided accommodation for pilgrims who came here in search of a cure. The cottage contained just one room on the ground floor with an attic above. There is evidence that there was a fireplace in the ground floor room and a door leading directly into the main well-chamber, although that doorway was subsequently blocked up.

Some distance away from this group of buildings there is an 18th century latrine. This lavatory was deliberately constructed over the stream which served as a natural sewer. Raised 18th century stone causeways link the well house and cottage to both the lavatory and the stone slab bridge which spans the stream. Writing in 1907, Myrddin Fardd stated that, during his life time, the cottage, Ty'n y Ffynnon, was inhabited. According to an article written in 1904 by William Williams each new tenant to Ty'n y Ffynnon had to pay the departing tenant the sum of £3 5s 0d. Ten shillings of this money was to pay for Llain y Ffynnon, the strip of land adjacent to the well, and the rest was for Llawr y Ffynnon, the floor of the well.

The 18th century buildings on the site were erected in the middle of the century. They were constructed by the owner of the land, William Price of Rhiwlas near Bala, whose intention it was to turn the site into a kind of spa where visitors could obtain cures for their illnesses. He was persuaded to make his investment on the advice of the Vicar of Llanystumdwy who informed him about the healing properties of the Llangybi well water. Apparently the vicar was aware that a certain Doctor Linden had carried out an analysis on a sample of the Llangybi well water and had published a pamphlet entitled *An Experimental and Practical Enquiry*. The doctor's researches confirmed that the water at Ffynnon Gybi possessed beneficial mineral properties. This, of course, was a time when 'taking the waters' was becoming increasingly fashionable at places like Bath in England and at certain spas in Wales.

This well had a reputation for curing 'warts, lameness, scrofula, scurvy and rheumatism', and Francis Jones records that during the 18th century, after people had been cured, 'crutches and wheelbarrows could be seen lying around the site.' (cited by Francis Jones *The Holy Wells of Wales*) Hyde-Hall, writing at the beginning of the 19th century, stated that Ffynnon Gybi was 'of much efficacy in scrofulous cases.' Scrofula was a form of tuberculosis of the neck, in which the lymph nodes became infected and then erupted into a mass of unsightly swellings. Writing in 1806 in his *Survey of Caernafonshire* William Williams of Llandegai also mentions this well: 'Here is a famous bath of cold spring water which is

140

much resorted to and esteemed in curing rheumatic pains and debilities of body... I have observed before that it is well known that a sudden plunge of the body into cold spring water does wonders in such complaints and divers other diseases.' He goes on to say that the waters of this spring are said to be saturated with a variety of minerals which the water assimilates from the hills above the spring.

A *Register of Cures*, dating from 1766, records that, after having bathed at this well, several people were either cured or afforded much relief from their afflictions. For example, it states that Shôn Rhydderch, a man who had been blind for 30 years, regained his sight after bathing his eyes at Ffynnon Gybi for three consecutive weeks, and that William Shôn Thomas, a Llangybi tailor, was cured of a sharp pain in his nose after treating it with water from this well. (*Arch. Camb.* 1904)

CADW states that patients, coming to this curative spa, would be given equal quantities of well-water and seawater to drink each morning and each evening for a period of seven to ten days. Then they were instructed to bathe in the well once or twice a day. Finally they were ordered to go to bed in the adjoining cottage where they were given well-water to drink. The efficacy of this treatment could be judged according to whether the patient became warm in bed or remained cold. If the patient became warm it was concluded that the treatment was having a positive effect.

Writing in 1904, local man William Williams, recorded that the late Mr. Francis Ellis had told him that it used to be the tradition for patients to cast pennies and silver coins into the water following each immersion, and that this money was gathered up regularly by the well keeper. This must have provided the owner of the site with a substantial income! Sometimes, at the end of their stay, patients would take containers of the healing water away with them for use at home.

The same author also reported that an 87 year old lady from the village once told him that she had lived in the house attached to the well during the 1870s. She also remembered visiting the well as a child of 7 early in the 19th century. She said that the basin, which was lined with blue slabs, was 3.5–4 feet deep. 'The ledge surrounding the water would be gay with primroses and other spring flowers, whilst the entrance was guarded by a graceful laburnum; the niches were full of books, and crutches were to be seen hanging on the side next to the house.' Apparently it used to be customary for the women of the village, after washing their clothes, to soak and swill them in the water of the gofer (the stream which runs away from the well) before putting them out to dry. (*Arch. Camb.* 1904)

There is a story told that one day a party of men were transporting some smuggled casks of spirits which they had collected from Porth Dinllaen, the most important smuggling port on the northern coast of Llŷn. The story goes on to tell how, on their way home, they were met by a Revenue or Excise man who demanded to know what they were carrying in the barrels. They replied that they had simply been to Saint Cybi's Well to fetch holy water for the well's owner, Mr William Price of Rhiwlas. Since such a practice was quite common at that time, it appears that their explanation was accepted and they were allowed to proceed on their way with their smuggled goods. (*Arch. Camb.* 1904)

Many years ago there was a widely held belief that an eel lived in this well, and it was considered to be an excellent sign if the eel coiled itself around the patient's bare limbs during bathing. One day a rumour was spread around the neighbourhood that a very large eel had been caught in Ffynnon Gybi and had been removed from the basin. This news caused considerable consternation locally as many of the old folk felt that the virtue of the well had been taken away with the removal of the eel. Fenton in his Tours of Wales 1804-13 refers to Ffynnon Gybi as a curative well although he makes no mention of the legendary eel.

It is said that the site of this well was a scene of great merriment and rejoicing at certain times of the year, such as 'Noswyliau Llawen and Gwyliau Mabsant'. (*Arch. Camb.* 1904) During the 19th century it was a tradition for all the girls of Llangybi and the surrounding area to gather at the well on the eve of Saint Cybi's Day. We cannot be sure why they gathered here, although it may have been a tradition which harked back to the wakes on medieval saints' days. It has also been said that this well was consulted regularly by girls who wished to know of their lovers' intentions. Sir John Rhŷs described the procedure thus, 'To discover the truth they would place a pocket handkerchief or a feather on top of the well water, and if the water pushed that object to the south they knew that everything was right and that their lovers were honest and honourable in their intentions; but if the water shifted it northwards, they were able to conclude to the contrary.' According to Myrddin Fardd, the water from this well was regularly used for baptisms in the local parish church.

Llangybi – Ffynnon Llywelyn

Like Ffynnon Gybi this well was a curative well, considered particularly effective for treating scrofula, a disease which produced unsightly swellings on the neck glands and which was also known as the King's Evil. For centuries it was commonly believed that the King's Evil could be cured if the patient was touched by the hand of a monarch. If no monarch was readily accessible people afflicted with scrofula would visit a well like Ffynnon Llywelyn or Ffynnon Gybi in the hope of being cured. The precise location of Ffynnon Llywelyn has not been found, although it is mentioned by Francis Jones and it is recorded on the database of historic monuments of North Wales. Nothing further is known about its history.

Llaniestyn – Ffynnon y Brenin

Originally Ffynnon y Brenin, which is situated in the parish of Llaniestyn near the summit of Garn Fadrun, may have been a sacred well associated with the Celtic tribespeople who built their Iron Age hill fort on top of the Garn. Subsequently this well achieved a reputation as a Christian healing well.

Ffynnon y Brenin, which was described by the AONB team in 2005 as being in good condition, was alleged to have been able to cure not only depression but also infertility. One or two other Llŷn wells also had a reputation for being able to treat infertility. In the past it was a commonly held belief that the water from certain holy wells could enable a childless woman to bear a child. It is recorded that, in 1663, King Charles II took his queen, Catherine of Braganza, to be treated at the wells in Bath so that she might be able to bear children.

The king referred to in the title 'Ffynnon y Brenin', is undoubtedly King Arthur, the legendary Romano-Celtic warrior-leader who battled to halt the advance of the invading Anglo-Saxons. Other local features of the landscape also refer to King Arthur – for example there is a very large flat stone on Garn Fadrun, called Bwrdd Arthur or Bwrdd y Brenin (Arthur's table or the King's table) and a prehistoric cromlech at Cefnamwlch, not far from Tudweiliog, called Coeten Arthur (Arthur's quoit).

According to literature, King Arthur lived during the late 5th or early 6th century although the historical basis for his existence has long been debated by historians. According to tradition Arthur was born at Tintagel Castle in Cornwall, the son of Uther Pendragon, a Celtic ruler. It is believed that an Iron Age settlement once existed on the headland where the early 13th century Tintagel castle was subsequently built. In about 600 Tintagel would have been a thriving port, trading in tin and copper. But to what extent Arthur's biographical details and the stories associated with him are true is open to question.

There is some evidence to suggest that an ancient leader, perhaps referred to as Arthur, did actually exist. In the 6th century the priest Gildas mentioned a warrior-leader called Ambrosius Aurelianus, who defeated the Saxons at the Battle of Mount Badon. There is a theory that the name Arthur meaning 'bear man' was a nickname given to Ambrosius Aurelianus because he was of exceptionally large build and wore a bearskin cloak, similar to those worn by Roman officers. Dr. Miles Russell points out that a poem called 'Y Gododdin', the earliest surviving piece of Welsh poetry dating from the end of the 6th century, 'compares one of its lead characters to Arthur, which suggests that he may have existed as a model of heroism by the start of the seventh century.' (Russell: *King Arthur's Legend*)

Much later, some 300 years after Arthur's probable death, the Welsh cleric, Nennius, mentioned Arthur by name in his *Historia Brittonum* (History of the Britons) in connection with his Mount Badon victory over the Saxons. One hundred years after Nennius an anonymous chronicler again names Arthur in the *Annales Cambriae* (The Annals of Wales) in connection with the victory at Mount Badon.

When he wrote his *Historia Regum Britanniae* (History of the Kings of Britain) in the 1130s, several centuries after the probable time of Arthur, Geoffrey of Monmouth romanticised this warrior's exploits. Imaginations were fired, and thereafter tales about Arthur became extremely popular. Medieval kings were also captivated by Arthur's heroic reputation. At Nefyn in the summer of 1284, Edward I staged a magnificent tournament based on the idea of King Arthur's Round Table. Down the centuries Arthur's popularity continued; his exploits not only captivated English kings but they were also popular in Wales and medieval France where tales about him were written. King Arthur was also popular with Tudor monarchs – Henry VII named his eldest son Arthur to reinforce his hold on the English throne, and at the courts of Henry VIII and Elizabeth I the tradition of Arthurian chivalry was very much in evidence. In Victorian times the Arthurian tradition continued to intrigue and inspire writers, poets and artists and it has continued to do so ever since.

As a warrior of Celtic origin King Arthur's story is closely associated with the Celtic areas of Britain and he is considered to be a great hero by Welsh people. His exploits and reputation were certainly very well known in Wales, for Arthur features in early Welsh literature. As indictated above, he is mentioned in the Welsh 6th century poem 'Y Gododdin'. He and his band of warriors are also identified in a Welsh story, 'Cullwch and Olwen', which was written down in the 12th century but which was almost certainly based upon material from the much earlier tradition of oral story telling. This tale was subsequently included in 'The Mabinogion', a collection of Middle Welsh texts which narrate heroic and mythological stories about Celtic Britain. Over time Arthur's life story became bound up with magic and he was associated with a close band of followers, who later featured in Arthurian legend as the Knights of the Round Table.

A theory put forward by two 20th century Welsh authors suggests that King Arthur fought this final battle of Camlan near Porth Cadlan in Llŷn. They suggest that, after he had been mortally wounded at Camlan, he was taken across the water to Ynys Enlli (*Bardsey*), which they claim is the Isle of Avalon of Arthurian legend. (Research by Barber & Pykitt 1993 cited by Elfed Gruffydd)

A much earlier source suggests a different version of events. Writing in the late 12th/early 13th century, Gerald of Wales, Archdeacon of Brecon, stated that, after King Arthur's death following the battle of Camlan, his body was buried 16 feet underground in the graveyard at Glastonbury Abbey on the Isle of Avalon. He stated that this was the ancient name for Glastonbury, then virtually an island surrounded by a river and marshland.

Gerald maintained that he had visited Arthur's grave after King Henry II had ordered it to be opened up in 1191. He reported that the grave contained of a wooden coffin, which was a 'hollowed-out oak-bole placed between two stone pyramids', and covered by a large stone slab, bearing a leaden cross, inscribed with the words, 'Here in the Isle of Avalon lies buried the renowned King Arthur, with Guinevere, his second wife.' Gerald also maintained that he personally examined the skull and the bones of the male person as they were removed from that grave. He records that they were of an immense size, much larger than those of most ordinary men. He also noticed that the relics bore evidence of many battle wounds. (Appendix 3 in Gerald's *Journey Through Wales and The Description Through Wales*)

King Henry did not live to see the results of this excavation, but in 1278, one of his successors, King Edward I issued instructions that the remains of Arthur and Guinevere should be reinterred within a black marble tomb in front of the high altar inside Glastonbury Abbey. Both the tomb and the abbey were destroyed at the time of the Reformation and there has been no trace of the bones since that time. Was this

Glastonbury burial really the grave of King Arthur or was it simply an elaborate hoax perpetrated by the abbot and the monks of Glastonbury in order to attract visitors to their abbey? We cannot be sure.

Although there is some evidence to suggest that there probably was a real Celtic leader who fought valiantly to repel the Saxons, the actual truth about his life and death remains unclear. One eminent historian has tentatively summed it up thus: 'Stirring legends of King Arthur grew up around the life of a relatively minor 5th or 6th century British or Welsh prince who fought against the advancing Saxons and who was perhaps the leader at a famous victory over the Saxons at Mount Badon.' (Charles Philips: *Kings & Queens of Britain*) It is possible that the medieval version of King Arthur is an amalgamation of more than one local tribal leader, including Ambrosius Aurelianus, whom the 6th century monk Gildas mentioned in his writings.

Whatever the historical facts, during the Middle Ages there was a firm belief, among kings and commoners alike, that King Arthur had been a real person who had fought heroically to halt the advance of the Saxons. For centuries he has been regarded as a courageous and chivalrous figure in Wales and indeed throughout Britain and France.

Ffynnon Y Brenin, is just one of several Welsh place-names which refer to King Arthur, and it is probably a medieval construction based upon the popular cult surrounding this shadowy and romanticised Romano-Celtic leader.

Llaniestyn – Ffynnon y Filast

The site of Ffynnon y Filast could not be located by the author and, since it does not lie within the Area of Oustanding Natural

Beauty it is not mentioned by the AONB team in their survey. It is, however, recorded on the database of North Wales ancient monuments and it is also mentioned by Myrddin Fardd, Francis Jones and the Pen Llŷn website. It was reputed to be a healing well and, according to Myrddin Fardd, it was capable of curing sore eyes, as well as melancholy and all manner of female complaints including infertility. In the past it was widely believed that the water from certain wells could enable infertile women to bear children, and there are documentary accounts, dating from the 16th century onwards, of women in Britain and Europe carrying out rituals at wells in the hope that they might be able to bear a child.

Llaniestyn – Pistyll y Garn

Like Ffynnon y Brenin, this well is also situated within the parish of Llaniestyn. It, too, is on the slopes of Garn Fadrun, and Myrddin Fardd records that, in the past, drinking its water was considered to be effective for the treatment of rheumatism as well as stomach and bowel problems. As has been mentioned before, the remains of an ancient fort and several hut circles are to be found on the Garn, and therefore, thousands of years ago, Pistyll y Garn may have been another natural spring associated with the ancient Iron Age people who lived here. The author has not located the exact position of this well.

Llanystumdwy – Ffynnon Betws Fawr

In a field near Betws Fawr Farm, north-west of the village of Llanystumdwy, there is an ancient well described by Francis Jones as having 'a wall of stones around it and an old ash tree nearby.' On the O.S. Explorer Map 254, south of Betws Fawr

Farm and west of the Afon Dwyfach, the position of this well is indicated by the word 'Well'. In 1960 RCAMHW described it as a stone structure cut into a slope and dry-built of fairly large boulders. They described the well as keyhole-shaped in plan with a well chamber about 1.22m in diameter, roofed by a large slab, which was overgrown. They reported that the water flowed from the well chamber into a tapering pool which measured about 3.66m long and which was 0.77m at its narrowest point, widening to 3.66m at its north-eastern end. This tapering pool was covered by slate slabs supported upon a narrow brick ledge built around the pool.

Nothing is known about the history of this well, but the name Betws (chapel or oratory) suggests a religious connection. A short distance to the north of the well between Betws Fawr and Betws Bach are the remains of an historic chapel as recorded on the OS Explorer Map. Although Myrddin Fardd mentioned Ffynnon Betws Fawr in his book of 1908, he makes no mention of any special properties associated with it. Close by, near the Afon Dwyfach, there is an ancient standing stone, probably dating from the Early Bronze period.

Llanystumdwy – Ffynnon Ddefaid

Situated within the parish of Llanystumdwy, Ffynnon Ddefaid was said by Francis Jones to be a healing well of great repute. Apparently its curative properties were first discovered by Richard Lewis, a gardener at the Plas Hen Estate (subsequently renamed the Talhenbont Hall Estate) when, in the 1770s, he bathed his sore eyes in its water. It seems that this well no longer exists, for Myrddin Fardd reported that it had already been destroyed when he published his book during the first decade of the 20th century.

Llanystumdwy – Ffynnon Gwaenydd

Pins are said to have been offered at this well which was reputed to be excellent for curing lameness. Francis Jones states that its curative properties were reputed to be so effective that, in days gone by, crutches which were no longer needed after treatment were left hanging on the branches of the nearby trees. Val Shepherd states that it was a common practice for people visiting this well to carve their names on the trees, as indeed they did at certain other Welsh wells. Apparently in 16th century Europe, many members of the nobility used to leave paintings or carvings of their coat of arms near wells as signs of their devotion to the saint. Perhaps the practice of name-carving on trees near wells served a similar purpose for the rural folk of Wales. The precise location of this well is not known.

Llwyndyrys – Ffynnon Gwynedd

The site of Ffynnon Gwynedd, which was probably a medieval holy well, is between Tyddyn Ffynnon and Penmaes, south of the village of Llwyndyrys. It was reputed to be able to cure arthritis and many other complaints. It was also said to have possessed the gift of prophecy. Sir John Rhŷs wrote, 'When it was desired to discover whether an ailing person would recover, one of his garments would be thrown into the well, and according to the side on which it sank it was known whether he would live or die.' As RCAHMW records, Ffynnon Gwynedd was originally '8 feet square, dry-built of large stones and raised 1 foot', but is now concreted over. However, some boulders are still visible at the sides below the level of the concrete, through which water exits via a modern pipe. The well is capped by slate slabs.

Mynytho – Ffynnon Fyw

Situated about 100 metres down the lane by the side of Capel Horeb in Mynytho, Ffynnon Fyw (*fyw*: live) was certainly a holy well. It was reputed to have been dedicated to Saint Curig, who is thought to have travelled extensively in Brittany, Cornwall and Wales and whose chapel, according to Baring-Gould and Fisher, once stood near this well, although there is certainly no trace of it today. Ffynnon Fyw, which is Grade II Listed, is generally considered to be one of the most interesting wells in Llŷn, owing to its unique structure and its prominent position. Myrddin Fardd called it 'an exceptional well'.

Ffynnon Fyw was described in an article published in the 1923 edition of *Archaeolgia Cambrensis* and again by RCAHMW in 1960. Set within a stone-walled enclosure 7.3 metres square, Ffynnon Fyw is unique because it has two adjacent basins, a larger one and a much narrower one. Originally the enclosing wall would probably have been 2m high or even a little higher. A narrow walkway separates the two basins and there is also a walkway around the interior of the outer wall. The larger basin was used for bathing, while the smaller of the two basins contained water for drinking.

The spring rises just outside the wall on the south side. There are stone seats built against the enclosing wall, stone steps leading down to the bathing pool at the southern corners of the east and west sides, and there is an entrance in the west wall. The main bathing pool, which is aligned north to south and which measures 3.66 metres by 2.74 metres, was reputed to be a healing well, especially beneficial for the treatment eye problems and blindness. In fact, in *Archaeologia Lleyn*, Daniel refers to blind people being completely cured at this well.

In the past, according to Myrrddin Fardd, a custodian who looked after the well would charge people a modest fee for instructing them in its use. Because of Ffynnon Fyw's special powers, as late as 1945 it is said that it was visited by a family from Birmingham in the hope that it would bring about the safe return of their two sons who had been reported missing during the Second World War. (Eirlys & Ken Gruffydd, cited on the Wellspring Internet site) Apparently they held a short service at the site and also made offerings at the well. Half a mile to the east of Ffynnon Fyw there is an ancient hut circle and enclosure, and there is evidence of an early defensive enclosure very near to the well at Gadlys.

There are several historical accounts relating to this well. Writing in the early years of the 19th century (1809-11) Edmund Hyde-Hall stated that Ffynnon Fyw was in a deplorable condition, for 'the external walls surrounding the well have recently been wantonly thrown down into the interior'. (Hyde-Hall *A Description of Caernarfonshire* He went on to say that, when he last visited this well about thirty years previously (i.e in about 1780), Mr. Assheton Smith of Faenol had repaired the broken-down walls and had fixed a new door to the structure. Hyde-Hall expressed the wish that 'another public benefactor came forward to restore this interesting relic of byegone days to its former state.' (Hyde-Hall: *A Description of Caernarfonshire*. He also noted that the well was situated upon an uncultivated 'rhos' or moorland (presumably a common) for he described the land around the well as being in a very poor state.

According to Samuel Lewis (*A Topographical Dictionary of Wales*) (writing in 1843), during the 18th century Ffynnon Fyw was a popular place for social gatherings on Sundays during the summer. Around this well crowds of folk took part in all kinds of rustic sports and ball games. This picture is confirmed by Carlisle who wrote of Ffynnon Fyw in 1811, 'Wakes were regularly kept in honour of it, when vast crowds of People met round the spot for three successive Sundays in July, where playing at Ball, and other country gambols were in great vogue.' Carlisle goes on to state that the practice of gathering there for games had died out some 40 years previously and 'the Well is now holden in no estimation.' (*Carlisle 'Topographical Dictionary of Wales*. This phrase supports Hyde-Hall's comment that the well had fallen into disuse and it probably explains why it had been vandalised so badly when he visited it for the second time early in the 19th century. The recreational pursuits described by Carlisle and Hyde-Hall may hark back to the traditional wakes which were often held at Welsh well sites on saints' feast days during the Middle Ages.

There is a story told that, on one occasion, a man threw a dead animal into Ffynnon Fyw, after which it was noticed that the well water appeared only during alternate years. This led members of the local population to believe that the spirit of the well, which had been offended by the pollution, had decided to inflict a punishment on all the well users.

In his *Topography of Wales* (1843) Lewis calls this well 'Ffynnon Dduw (God's Well) near Llanbedrog' and Carlisle (writing in 1811) also refers to it as Ffynnon Dduw. However, it is clear from Lewis's description that he was referring to Ffynnon Fyw at Mynytho. Since Mynytho is not very far away from Llanbedrog, this well must have been known by both names. It was not uncommon for certain Welsh wells to have more than one name.

We have seen that this well was repaired by Mr Assheton Smith of Faenol in the second half of the 18th century. Apparently it was restored again in 1890. Some amateur renovation work was carried in the late 1950s, but when it was inspected in 2002 the site was in an appalling condition – the ancient stone walls were crumbling and the well basins themselves were rapidly disappearing under a profusion of vegetation. When the AONB team visited Ffynnon Fyw at the beginning of the 21st century they reported that it 'needed attention and had grown very wild'. In about 2005 the well was completely cleared and restored by the AONB team. Shortly after its restoration when the author visited it the site was in excellent condition but when he visited it for a second time in 2015 the vegetation had invaded again and the well was in danger of becoming completely overgrown.

Mynytho – Ffynnon Sarff

Ffynnon Sarff is to be found at the north-western edge of Mynytho Common. It can be reached by taking the unclassified road which leads from the B4413 towards Foel Bach and then by walking for about 100 metres down the path beside the wood called Gwinllan Sarff. There is no stonework associated with this well, for it is simply a spring which emerges out of the ground before disappearing under an adjacent wall and flowing down hill through the pine woods. The source of the spring is covered by a lid, unfortunately broken when inspected by the author, causing the water to be unclean.

As its name suggests Ffynnon Sarff was believed to have been guarded by a serpent. In years gone by many people claimed to have seen this creature at the well, although Myrddin Fardd suggested that they had probably chanced upon a snake which had come from a nearby nest to drink. Little is known about the history of Ffynnon Sarff. However, since there was believed to be a guardian serpent, one would suspect that it was reputed to have had some special properties, possibly of a curative nature, although no documentation about its extraordinary powers has been found.

Just over half a mile to the north west of Ffynnon Sarff,

situated above the slopes of the Nanhoron Valley at Pandy Saethon there is a standing stone, while nearer still there is evidence of house platforms and an ancient homestead.

Mynytho – Ffynnon Saethon

Not far away from Ffynnon Sarff is an ancient well called Ffynnon Saethon which is situated north-west of Rhedyn at the south-western end of the track which leads to it from the drive to Saethon Farm. Considered by RCAHMW to be a possible medieval well, Ffynnon Saethon is situated close to Garn Saethon where there are the remains of an Iron Age stone fort. As RCAHMW states, all that exists of the well today is a rough rectangle of boulders about 1 metre square which is cluttered with stones. Today there is no evidence of a clear spring, for there is just a stagnant pool of water, filled with debris. There seems to be evidence of a retaining wall about 0.92m feet square, and there may be evidence of a larger surround of masonry measuring approximately 2.44m by 1.83m. Originally, on the north-western side, there appear to have been steps leading down to the water.

It is said that, a long time ago, Ffynnon Saethon was visited by pilgrims. It is recorded by Sir John Rhys that, later on, it was frequented by lovers who sought help in foretelling the future. A young lover would pluck thorns from a nearby thorn tree and cast them into the water. If the thorns floated it was seen as a good sign that their love was steadfast; if the thorns whirled around it was an indication that her partner was of a cheerful disposition; if the thorns sank a little way under the surface of the water but could still be seen the young man was said to be awkward and bad-tempered; but if the thorns sank out of sight it was considered terrible news and therefore time to look elsewhere.

According to Francis Jones, there is documentary evidence to show that members of the Saethon family came regularly to this well from the large house nearby to bathe in both summer and winter, so beneficial were the waters considered to be.

Mynytho – Ffynnon Arian

Situated east of Foel Gron and west of the main road which runs through Mynytho, Ffynnon Arian is reputed to be a wishing well. This well is marked on the O.S. Explorer Map 253 with a 'W'. The well is described by RCAHMW as 'A natural spring, possibly medieval, with no traces of structure.' In 2005 the AONB team reported that this well had 'clean water with a tidy lid.' Francis Jones records that some Welsh wells were connected to stories of treasure and so, on account of its name, he says that Ffynnon Arian may have been associated with a treasure tale. (Francis Jones: *The Holy Wells of Wales* p. 134) There is, however, no firm evidence to support this theory. Nothing further is known about the history of this well.

Mynytho (Foel Fawr) – Ffynnon Fair

Situated on the slope of Foel Fawr about 1 mile due east of Llanbedrog, Ffynnon Fair was described by the RCAHMW as a three-cornered well with a basin measuring 2.4 metres by 1.3 metres on a north-west to south-east alignment, although it has been substantially modernised. Access to it is steep and quite difficult. Because it is dedicated to the Virgin Mary it must have been a holy well. It was said to have possessed extraordinary healing properties, for local tradition suggests that it was capable of treating all kinds of human and animal complaints.

Myrddin Fardd states that it also possessed the power of prophecy, enabling it to reveal the identity of a thief. First, the injured party had to kneel before the well to profess his or her faith. Then, as was the case at Ffynnon Bedrog, pieces of bread were thrown into the well, one at a time, whilst at the same time calling out the name of each suspect in turn. If one of the pieces of bread sank to the bottom of the well the person named was the guilty party. As mentioned previously, this is reminiscent of the medieval practice of trial by water, except that, in the Middle Ages, it was not a piece of bread that was thrown into water to float or sink but the person who was suspected of committing the crime! As alluded to earlier, casting bread into a spring is also mentioned in a 6th century letter written by Martin of Braga and, although the reason for this Celtic ritual is not explained, it must have been a fairly common practice among the Celtic peoples.

Mynydd Mynytho – Holy Well

Francis Jones refers to a well called Holy Well, which he says is situated on farmland belonging to Holy Well Farm, on the south-western slopes of Mynydd Mynytho. He does not provide any further information about its use or its history. This well was not recorded by the AONB team but it is mentioned on the database of ancient monuments for North Wales. Nothing further is known about Holy Well. On the O.S. maps of the area the author was not able to locate either Holy Well Farm or a well on the south-western slopes of Mynydd Mynytho. If Holy Well did formerly exist its name suggests that, once upon a time, it must have had some religious significance.

Nefyn – Ffynnon Mynydd Nefyn

The AONB report describes Ffynnon Mynydd Nefyn as a 'strong structure with a gate, in good condition and with clean, pure water'. In days gone by, this was one of the main sources of domestic water for the community of people living on the mountain above Nefyn. From the centre of Nefyn the well can be reached by leaving Y Groes and proceding down Stryd y Plas. By the large car park next to the abandoned Capel Seion bear left and continue up the hill towards Mynydd Nefyn. The hill is quite steep and the road is fairly narrow with only a few passing places. At the top of the hill turn sharp left onto a minor unclassified road which leads across the Mynydd towards Gwylwyr Mountain. After a few yards along this road, take a track to the left, passing a dwelling called Cae Mawr. Walk past Cae Mawr and, on your right, you will notice an overgrown grassy path leading up the slope. The well is located at the top of this path about 20 metres above the road. There is no known record that this well was ever a holy or healing well or that it was considered to possess any special powers.

When the author visited this well he found it to be enclosed within a low, rectangular roofed stone-built well-house, measuring 2.1m across the front, 2.4m deep from front to back and 1.5 m high at the front. Its flat roof, which is formed of large thick slabs of slate, slopes down from front to back. A piece of stone embedded across the entrance forms a lip across the threshold and beyond this lip, inside the well-house, are two stone steps which originally afforded access to the water. The entrance opening, which measures 1.23m high by 0.6m wide, faces SSE and is now protected externally by a galvanised metal gate. There was a plentiful supply of clear water inside the well house when the author inspected it, although a couple of large ferns were growing against the interior rear wall.

Nefyn – Ffynnon Fair

As its name suggests, Ffynnon Fair is dedicated to the Virgin Mary although, like the town itself, it was probably associated with an early Celtic saint, possibly the 5th century Saint Nyfain, one of the daughters of Brychan. Ffynnon Fair must have been an early Christian holy well for Nefyn was a very early settlement and it is believed that a settlement with a 'llan' or Christian burial ground was established here at the time of the Celtic Saints.

The fresh water supply provided by Ffynnon Fair was undoubtedly instrumental in the establishment of a settlement here. The well is situated in the centre of the town just below the cross roads (Y Groes) at the top of Stryd y Ffynnon. Since Nefyn and its well lay at a strategic point, half way along the peninsula on the pilgrim route to Enlli, it would undoubtedly have been an important pilgrim well. As its name suggests it would also have been looked upon as a holy well. It is a Grade 2 listed structure.

Henry Parry states that before the present stone structure was built over the well in the middle of the 19th century, this Nefyn well-site used to be considerably larger. He states that the well was once surrounded by a wall about 10 feet high but roofless. Internally the basin measured about '4 yards by 5 yards' and access to it was via a quaint archway which faced down Stryd y Ffynnon towards Pen isa'dre. Surrounding the well basin there were stone seats where people could rest, and in the walls which enclosed the well there were a number of recesses. This design is similar to that of several other prominent Llŷn holy wells. Such a design suggests that this well was not only a holy well and a source of domestic water for the town's inhabitants but it must also have been a healing well where people could access the water to bathe. Henry Parry states that when the new well-house was built none of the stones from the previous structure were reused. (Henry Parry: *History of Nefyn and District*) There is no record of the ailments which this well was reputed to be able to treat.

Ffynnon Fair was rebuilt in its present form in the mid 19th century, almost certainly to protect the town's water supply at a time when epidemics of water- borne diseases were becoming increasingly common. The well house, which is built of blocks of local ashlar granite, is square in plan with shallow false arched recesses on each of its four sides. The granite roof is in the form of a pyramid, each face bearing a triangular, inscribed slate panel. These panels record that the Nefyn Town Corporation erected this building over the well in 1868, that Lord Newborough was the Mayor of Nefyn, that Hugh Hughes was the Deputy Mayor, that John Wilson was the town's Recorder, and that Robert Thomas and John Jones were the town's Bailiffs.

Ffynnon Fair was the town's domestic water supply until 1906, when the Lleyn Rural District Council constructed a small reservoir on Mynydd Nefyn from where water was piped into the town. To one side of the well building, adjacent to Canton House (the former Post Office), there is a sunken area where water from the spring flows out through a large tap at the base of the well-house wall. There is a large metal grille beneath the tap to take away any surplus water flowing from the tap. This sunken area, which is accessed from the pavement by means of a set of steps, is enclosed by iron railings and an iron gate which faces the road.

Today Ffynnon Fair retains a strong flow of water which, upon leaving the well- house, runs in an underground drain at the side of Stryd y Ffynnon. The outflow of water can be viewed beneath several slotted drain covers as it flows down the hill towards the river at the end of Stryd y Felin.

The names of several of the properties at the top of Stryd y Ffynnon indicate their proximity to this well – Min y Ffynnon, Ael y Ffynnon, Maes y Ffynnon and Uwch y Ffynnon. The street (Stryd y Ffynnon) and the nearby café behind the former Post Office (Caffi'r Ffynnon) are also named after it.

Nefyn – Ffynnon John Morgan

This well is to be found on the hillside above Nefyn, beneath the small abandoned quarry known as Gwaith John Lloyd. To locate it proceed from Y Groes down Stryd y Plas and, at the fork in the road opposite the car park, take the road to the left which leads up onto Mynydd Nefyn. As you ascend the steep hill, on the left hand side of the road, there is a large, field-type metal gate which affords access to a track. This track heads in the direction of a dwelling called Tan y Mynydd, the name of which is clearly displayed beside the metal gate. About half way along this track is Ffynnon John Morgan. It was totally overgrown when visited by the author and the AONB team. It probably provided the domestic water for the nearby dwellings although no record could be been found relating to its history. It is not known if it was reputed to have had any special powers.

Nefyn – Ffynnon Pin y Wig

Ffynnon Pin y Wig could not be located by the ANOB team nor by the author. It is simply recorded by Francis Jones as a 'rill in Nefyn parish'. He may have been referring to the stream which flows down from the Fron, past the old Saint Mary's Church and under the bridge at the end of Stryd y Felin. However, this is simply guesswork. Myrddin Fardd stated that Ffynnon Pin y

Wig was used for healing people's sore hands and knuckles. He also states that local farmers sometimes took their cows to this well to be treated if they had warts on their udders.

Nefyn – Ffynnon Gybi Bach

This well is mentioned in the online Snowdon Heritage Leaflet, simply indicating that it was located 'on the western side of Ty'n Coed, but has now disappeared to all intents and purposes.' Nothing further is known about this well or its history.

Penarth near Aberdesach – Ffynnon Ddigwg

This well is near Penarth in the Aberdesach area and an article in *Archaeologia Cambrensis* states that Ffynnon Ddigwig is situated 'on the hillside'. Although this well has not been visited by the author, he noticed on the O.S. Explorer Map 254 that a spring is shown on higher ground to the south west of Penarth and a little to the north east of Gilfach. This may be Ffynnon Ddigwig, although this is by no means certain. A burial cairn and the remains of a Neolithic tomb can be seen nearby.

In the 1960s the RCAHMW recorded that Ffynnon Ddigwig 'survives merely as a large marshy hollow with no visible ancient structure.' Francis Jones states that there are several historical reports which refer to people seeing strange objects in this well. He says that a manuscript in the National Library of Wales records that one elderly female resident said she had noticed, lying at the bottom of the well, objects which looked like oranges, and that nobody had managed to pull one to the surface. He also mentions that other local people claimed to have seen creatures which looked like 'hedgehogs without any spikes' living in the well.

Myrddin Fardd recorded that, Eben Fardd (1802-1863) the poet and schoolmaster at Clynnog, had stated that this well was also called Ffynnon Gwttig or Gyttig. Apparently water from this well was renowned for curing warts. It was the practice to offer both pins and eggs to the well in order to bring about an effective treatment.

There are several tales associated with this well, including a legend about a hawthorn tree, a treasure story and a ghost tale. Francis Jones mentions a local superstition which stated that if an old hawthorn tree growing near the well was ever chopped down catastrophic thunder and lightning would erupt. Myrddin Fardd says that another strange locally-held belief was that money hidden at the well would be revealed to nobody apart from 'a red-haired girl who looked after sheep'. There was also a local tale about the ghost of a wailing child which haunted a field near Ffynnon Ddigwig. This legend is similar to a story associated with Ffynnon Grasi at Glasfryn. One is left wondering how such strange stories originated! Several other Welsh wells are associated with stories of ghosts and treasure.

There are two very different legends which purport to explain how this well acquired its name. There is an ancient tale which recounts how Digwig, the daughter of King Ynyr of Gwent fell in love with a lowly, Anglesey-born workman who was carrying out some repairs at the king's palace. Eventually the king gave his blessing for the young workman to marry his daughter.

After the wedding, as the young couple were travelling by way of Clynnog Fawr to visit the bridegroom's home on Anglesey, they rested for the night near Penarth. During the night the young man became increasingly worried about the prospect of his princess visiting the humble home where he had been born and brought up. He decided that he would resolve the matter by cutting off her head with his sword as she slept. The foul deed having been done, Digwig's blood poured onto the ground and a spring, known today as Ffynnon Ddigwig, immediately began to issue forth from the ground which had been turned red by her blood. Having solved the problem of his embarrassment the young man left Digwig's body where it lay.

By good fortune, so the story says, Saint Beuno happened to pass that way. Noticing the severed head and the lifeless body of the young princess lying on the ground, he immediately reunited them and miraculously brought her back to life. Instantly the restored princess made up her mind that she would not return to her family in Gwent but instead decided to become one of Saint Beuno's disciples. There are a number of slight variations to this story.

Revd A.W. Wade-Evans suggests in *Archaeologia Cambrensis* Vol. LXXXV Part 2 that Ffynnon Ddigwig may be named after Tygwy, the brother of Saint Baglan, the founder of Llanfaglan. He says that Tygwy and Baglan were both cousins of Saint Beuno. Readers must decide for themselves which of the two explanations they find more interesting!

Pentrefelin – Ffynnon Ddunawd

This well is situated high above and behind the village of Pentrefelin in a field belonging to Braich y Saint Farm. To visit Ffynnon Ddunawd take the main road from Pwllheli to Porthmadog and, just before you enter the village of Pentrefelin turn left near a sign which advertises accommodation at Tyddyn Iolyn. Having turned onto this road you will pass some houses on the right, after which the road narrows. Take the next turning left and proceed along this very narrow lane until you come to a much more open area near the entrance to Braich Y Saint Farm. Ffynnon Ddunawd is in a field on the same side of the road as the farm immediately inside the field hedge which borders the road. This well is situated about 450 feet above sea level beneath a modern communication mast. It is marked by name on the O. S. Explorer Map No. 254.

Thousands of years ago Ffynnon Ddunawd may have been associated with an Iron Age tribe, for W. J. Hemp FSA mentions that an ancient hill fort once stood on the higher ground above Cae'r Dyni although it is 'now destroyed.' *Arch. Camb.* Vol IV Series 7

Today the well is enclosed within a stone-walled structure which is built into a steep bank adjoining the boundary wall of the field. Adjacent to the well there are also barely discernable traces of a long, rectangular building, the purpose of which is not clear. Could it have been an ancient well chapel? Inside this building the ground level falls away to the south towards the road, and its walls are largely destroyed although it is still just possible to determine the original extent and shape of this structure. At its western end there appears to have been an entrance which had been blocked up.

The well itself, which is also rectangular in shape, has been cut back into the steeply sloping ground, and was originally attached at its north-western corner to the stonework of the rectangular building. However, there is no evidence that there was once direct access between the well and the attached building. The well chamber itself is constructed of large flat-faced stones and boulders to a height of about four feet although the rear wall is certainly higher, probably about 5 feet.

The well itelf is fenced off from the rest of the field with a metal farm gate, which is secured across the entrance, but the well-site is extremely overgrown with brambles and weeds. When visited by the author he was scarcely possible to see the water in the well through the profusion of vegetation. Coflein states that a sill stone at the entrance to the well allows a maximum depth of about 1 foot of water although, when the author visited, it was not possible to see the sill on account of the undergrowth.

According to Baring-Gould & Fisher and the National Biography of Wales Saint Dunawd was originally a 6th century tribal chieftain from the north of Britain. It is said that he was forced to flee south where he was granted some land on the banks of the river Dee. Here in about 560 he and his sons, including Deiniol (who subsequently founded the abbey at Bangor, Gwynedd), established the monastery at Bangor is y Coed, Wrexham, where Ddunawd became the first abbot. Writing early in the 8th century the Venerable Bede states that Dunawd was still the abbot at Bangor is y Coed in about 602. He is believed to have died round about 607. The monastery was subsequently destroyed circa 616 by Aethelfrith of King of Northumbria and many of the monks were slaughtered, although it is believed that some escaped and made their way to Enlli.

It is said that Saint Cadfarch, whose name is associated with Abererch, was formerly at Saint Dunawd's monastery at Bangor is y Coed. We can only speculate as to why this Llŷn well was dedicated to Saint Dunawd. Ffynnon Ddunawd was obviously a holy well – perhaps also a healing well – although no further documentation has been found about its history. Traditionally it is said to have been one of the wells used by pilgrims as they followed the southern pilgrim route to Ynys Enlli.

Pentrefelin – Ffynnon Tyddyn Iolyn

Situated about 350 yards to the north of the same road on which Ffynnon Ddunawd lies but a little further to the east, is Ffynnon Tyddyn Iolyn which is located to the south of the dwelling named Tyddyn Iolyn Isaf. On the O.S. Explorer Map

254 it is marked by the letters 'Spr'. Apparently this well was renowned for its crystal clear water which was never too cold in winter and never too warm in summer. There is no evidence to suggest that it was ever considered to be a holy well. Ffynnon Tyddyn Iolyn must have been the water supply for the nearby dwellings although it is said that, many years ago, people also visited it to bathe their sore eyes.

Pistyll – Ffynnon Sanctaidd

Ffynnon Sanctaidd is situated about 150 metres east-south-east of Saint Beuno's Church, parts of which date back to the 12th century. This spring was probably a holy well associated with this ancient Church. Today Pistyll's historic and atmospheric little church nestles in a secluded spot between the main road and the coast.

The small settlement of Pistyll lies on the B4417 which leads from Nefyn to Llanaelhaearn, and it is said that its church was founded as a place of retreat and solitude for Saint Beuno himself. There is firm evidence of Christian activity in the Pistyll area in the 8th to 9th century, for a stone, believed to be of that date and inscribed with a cross inside a circle, is located in the hedge by the side of the road opposite the lay-by on the Nefyn to Llanaelhaearn road.

A community of monks was established near the original church, and Pistyll became an important resting place for medieval pilgrims travelling to Enlli. Around the church grew a variety of plants from which the monks made medicines. Some of those herbs can still be found growing in the churchyard. Ffynnon Sanctaidd is simply a natural spring which is now covered by a modern concrete slab. The verdict of the ANOB team was that it was in need of restoration and demodernisation. This well has none of the man-made walls, seats and walkways which characterise some of the more impressive Llŷn holy wells.

Ffynnon Sanctiadd is clearly an ancient well which has been associated with Christian activity for centuries, for it is known locally as the "Holy Well". It is said that, during the 20th century, water from this well was used for baptisms in Saint Beuno's Church at Pistyll.

Pistyll – Ffynnon Fednant

Francis Jones describes Ffynnon Fednant as 'a former healing well located near Nantypistyll', although he makes no mention of the ailments which it was reputed to cure. Situated at the the head of the beach at Porth Pistyll on the seaward side of Pistyll Farm, Ffynnon Fednant was said by Myrddin Fardd to ebb and flow with the tide. After leaving the source of the spring, the outflow flows across the beach towards the sea. This spring is clearly marked on the O.S. Explorer Map 253 by the letters 'Spr'.

Many years ago, according to Myrddin Fardd, this well was used in the performance of magic, when a local wizard, who lived in a cottage called Llwyn Ffynnon (on the eastern side of Moel-Ty-Gwyn), used water from this well in order to practise his sorcery. Nothing further is known about the history of Ffynnon Fednant. On the O.S. Explorer Map, the site of an ancient 'homestead' is marked nearby.

Pistyll – Ffynnon Cefnydd

Built by the community of monks at Pistyll, a medieval hospice was established on Cefnydd Hill in fields referred to locally as

Cae Hosbis (*hospice*) and Cae Hosbis Pennia. This was the place where sick pilgrims, including lepers, were cared for. Nothing remains of the former hospice now. The little church at Pistyll became the hospice church, complete with leper window through which the afflicted were able to see the altar and receive communion without having to set foot inside the building. The font in the church dates from the Age of the Saints.

To reach Ffynnon Cefnydd the visitor must go down the small lane towards Saint Beuno's church and, at the footpath sign, climb over the stile and follow the path at the edge of the field until you come to a track. Follow this track up the hill towards the ridge and head towards the farm called Cefnydd Farm. Ffynnon Cefnydd is a natural spring (marked 'Spr' on the O.S. Explorer Map 253) at the top of a steep slope near where a foot bridge crosses the stream. Cefnydd Farm is a little further up the hill. Myrddin Fardd states that, in times past, people came to this well seeking relief from arthritis, for which its water was reputed to be a very effective treatment.

No other information is known about the history of Ffynnon Cefnydd, but hundreds of years ago it was probably not only thought to be a healing well but it must have also provided a supply of fresh water for the nearby medieval hospice.

Porthmadog – Ffynnon Lôn Cei

Ffynnon Lôn Cei is situated along Lôn Cei near the slipway. Apparently years ago it was customary for people to go to this well to bathe their eyes.

Other Wells in the Porthmadog Area

Writing in 1856 Morris stated that Porthmadog lacked a dependable supply of water for domestic purposes. This caused many complaints and a great deal of hardship during the summer months 'when the two springs and stream on which the inhabitants depend are partly exhausted or dried up. The servants sent to draw water are kept waiting for hours – sometimes through a great part of the night – thus causing a heavy and pecuniary loss and inconvenience to the families.' (Morris: *Portmadoc and its Resources*) He goes on to state that if pipes were laid from the spring at Beudy'rychain to the square in Porthmadog the problem would be solved 'both cheaply and effectually.' Ffynnon Beudy'rychain was described in 1856 as a powerful spring 1100 yards from the town on the road to Cricieth.

Other ancient named wells in and around Porthmadog include Ffynnon Morfa Lodge (near the Catholic Church), Ffynnon Samson (near the golf course), Ffynnon Moel y Gest (near the side gate to the public cemetery) and Ffynnon Sam Richards (an old spring which issued from the rocks near the four most westerly Porthmadog quays, where some ships often used to fill their tanks and casks, thus saving 'the halfpenny per gallon... charge made by the Port Authorities.') (Hughes: *Immortal Sails*)

There are many other named wells in the Gest and Porthmadog areas. They include Ffynnon Eisteddfa; Ffynnon Cefn y Meusydd Isa (which was reputed to be excellent for treating animals suffering from constipation); Ffynnon Carreg y Felin; Ffynnon Ddiog; Ffynnon Fyw (nearly always full of water); Ffynnon Ty Coch (near Cross Keys, Pentrefelin); Ffynnon Tyddyn Engan, Treflys, (which serviced three nearby farms with water); Ffynnon Rhianod (on the bare slope at Bron y Foel); Ffynnon Cefn Cyfanedd; Ffynnon Brynmelyn; three different wells at Du Hwnt i'r Bwlch; Ffynnon Nant Adda (Penamser – by the cemetery); Ffynnon Dyddyn Adi; Ffynnon Llidiart yr Ysbyty (Tremadog); Ffynnon Cil Llidiart (behind the Madog Arms Hotel, Tremadog); Ffynnon Penrhynheli (Tanrallt), Ffynnon Corlan y Geifr (Tanrallt), Ffynnon Ynyscynhaearn (where the water was said to be medicinal), Ffynnon Bryn y Garth (Bron y Garth) and Ffynnon Tyddyneithin (near Borth y Gest). Many of the above wells were simply used as sources of domestic water. (Details of these wells have been taken taken from information written by Alltud Eifion)

It is reported that sometimes, when the Porthmadog wells had dried up, people would walk many miles to the wells in Gest, like those at Du Hwnt i'r Bwlch, to obtain water.

Pwllheli/Efail Newydd – Ffynnon Felin Bach

Ffynnon Felin Bach (*Felin Bach*: little mill) is located between Pwllheli and Efailnewydd on the road called Penlon Llŷn which runs from the crossroads at the end of the High Street in the centre of Pwllheli before joining the A497 road to Nefyn opposite the boundary wall of Plas Bodegroes. The well is situated on the left hand side of Penlon Llŷn (when travelling away from Pwllheli) on the corner where the road bends slightly to the left. The mill, after which the well is named, can be seen at the end of the lane on the opposite side of the road. There is no recorded tradition of healing or other special powers associated with this well, although it was used as a source for domestic water.

More recently this well achieved considerable notoriety on account of a poem written by Sir Albert Evans Jones, whose bardic name was Cynan. Born in Pwllheli in 1895 he was one of the great Welsh literary and National Eisteddfod figures of the 20th century. His poem 'Mab y Bwthyn', which won the crown at the National Eisteddfod tells how, during his service on the Western Front during the Great War, memories of this well would come flooding back to him. From time to time he would remember how, as a young lad, he often lay beside this well, dreaming his time away, while the pure, clear water from the well flowed over the sides of his grandmother's jug. One can easily imagine that, amidst the horror of that conflict, thoughts of his boyhood in Llŷn would come rushing back to him, causing him once again to be overcome by an intense longing for the cool, refreshing water of Ffynnon Felin Bach.

In 1967 the Friends of Pwllheli arranged for a retaining wall to be built behind the well (to prevent the bank from collapsing into the water), and for a slate plaque to be placed above it, inscribed with the name of the well and two lines from Cynan's poem:

Does dim wna f'enaid blin yn iach
Ond dŵr o Ffynnon Felin Bach.

(Nothing can refresh my troubled soul but water from the well of Felin Bach)

Other Pwllheli Wells

In days gone by the people of Pwllheli were adequately supplied with water, for there were several natural springs dotted around the town. Elfed Gruffydd states that none was known to be a healing well or to possess any special powers for, as far as we know, the Pwllheli wells were simply used as sources of domestic water. D.G. Lloyd Hughes in *Hanes Tref Pwllheli* has written in considerable detail about the old wells of the town.

The most important of the old Pwllheli wells were: Ffynnon Tan-y-clawdd (Stryd Moch), Ffynnon-y-bracty (Pentrepoeth later, in the vicinity of North Street), Ffynnon Penlan, Ffynnon Stryd y Farchnad (Market Street) and Ffynnon-yr-Onnen (Stryd Kingshead a'r Gors). Later on several others were brought into use for, during the second half of the 19th century, wells were opened in Caernarfon Road, Upper Terrace, Sand Street and Salem Terrace.

For many years the Pwllheli wells were 'open' springs where the water could be easily accessed, but during the 18th century pumps were fitted to some of them in order to safeguard the cleanliness of the water. At certain wells, even after pumps had been fitted, the water could still be accessed without using the pumps. At these wells people continued to cause problems by dumping rubbish into the well water and by washing dirty items in it. An unpleasant smell began to emerge from some of the town's wells and, when the smell was investigated at one Pwllheli well, the putrifying remains of a child's body were discovered in the water.

In the 1870s a Manchester company brought piped water to some of the houses from Mur Cwymp which is situated on higher ground some distance away to the north of Y Ffor. However, it took another 20 years for most of the houses in Pwllheli to be connected to the piped supply. Even then, some inhabitants still preferred to use the old wells instead of paying for piped water.

Tudweiliog – Ffynnon Gwyfan

Situated about a mile from Tudweiliog village, and lying between Twywn and Porth Ysgaden, Ffynnon Gwyfan is a D-shaped well which nestles at the foot of a rock above a small river. The rock which protects the well on its southern side, leans over it to provide a sort of protective canopy above it. Ffynnon Gwyfan was a healing well, for it had the reputation of being able to cure a variety of ailments including warts, ague and eye problems. Traditionally pins were thrown into the water in order to ensure a successful treatment. Although the name of the village of Tudweiliog clearly suggests some kind of association with Saint Tudwal the parish church is dedicated to Saint Cwyfan and Saint Brigit. As its name indicates, Ffynnon Gwyfan is also dedicated to Saint Cwyfan, who it is believed was of Irish origin and who seems to have been one of the followers of Saint Beuno. As suggested by the AONB team, this well is not easily accessible although its water is clean.

Tudweiliog – Ffynnon Porth Ysgaden

Ffynnon Porth Ysgaden was reported by the AONB team to be in good condition when they carried out their survey. The author has not located this well for no well or spring could be found on the O.S. map in the vicinity of Porth Ysgaden. Nothing further is known about it.

Tudweiliog – Ffynnon Penllech

In his book entitled *Ynys Enlli*, H.D. Williams states that this well was one of the stopping places for pilgrims en route to Enlli although it is not recorded by Francis Jones, Myrddin Fardd or the AONB team. Its precise location remains a mystery.

Rhiw – Ffynnon Cwm-dylif

There are several ancient wells in the vicinity of Rhiw. Myrddin Fardd tells us that 'from the top of the steep hill which leads to the village of Rhiw we can actually see no fewer than five holy wells, and some of them are notable ones.' (cited by R. Gerallt Jones)

Ffynnon Cwm-dylif is situated beneath Mynydd Rhiw on its western side in Nant Meillionydd, and it is marked by name on the O. S. Explorer map No. 253. Writing in 1799, Ieuan Lleyn (1769-1832) mentioned Cwm Dylif in his *Jouney through Lleyn*. 'I travelled ahead leaving Hirwaun and Plas Newydd on the right and Bodwyddog and Meillionydd on the left until at last I reached the source of the river at Cwm Dylif, on Meillionydd land. The river flows from an underground stream over a trough that looks man made, although it is natural.'

On the hillside above the well, Ieuan Lleyn also mentioned the ruined remains of an old church or chapel, which he refers to as Capel Cwm Dylif. It is not known if the well was associated with the ancient chapel above it or if its water was believed to have possessed any special powers, for nothing further is known about its history. In the distant past Ffynnon Cwm-dylif may have been associated with the double ring enclosure at Bryn Meillion which dates from the late Bronze Age/early Iron Age and which is situated on the higher ground above the well. At the time of writing the Bryn Meillion site was being excavated by archaeologists from Bangor University.

Rhiw – Ffynnon Aelrhiw

Ffynnon Aelrhiw, which is Grade II Listed, was refurbished by the AONB team a few years ago but unfortunately it has been seriously invaded again by a mass of brambles and other dense vegetation.

The well is situated in a field about 150 metres to the south-west of the church in Rhiw, and it can be reached by going through the field gate opposite the church and heading across the field. Within 360m of this well there is a long burial cairn to the north east and a burial chamber to the south west and, long ago, this well may have been associated with those nearby prehistoric sites. The area around Rhiw is particularly rich in prehistoric remains.

Ffynnon Aelrhiw consists of a stone walled enclosure which is approximately 3.6 metres square and which is built of coursed boulders. It has a rectangular basin, surrounded by a stone walkway and continuous stone seats around three sides. The basin is accessed by means of low steps on the northern side and higher steps on the eastern side. In the northern corner of the wall is a small niche about 28 cm. deep. The entire structure is set into a SE facing steep slope, and the stonework on the northwest side forms a retaining wall to hold back the ground above it. The remaining walls are now incorporated into modern field walls. The entrance, on the northern flank, is marked by a tall upright stone on one side and a step. In the north-eastern corner of the wall there is a small niche. A post and wire fence surrounds the whole site. An iron gate affords access to it and a slate signpost indicates the well's presence.

Although the spring cannot be seen through the mass of vegetation, the spring itself is still active for a steady stream of water can be seen flowing away from the site, down the hill and across the field. In days gone by this stream powered the mill which stood above the 17th century manor house of Plas yn Rhiw.

During the Middle Ages when pilgrimages were commonplace Ffynnon Aelrhiw, like so many others, was one of the stopping places for people making their way to Enlli along the southern route. One can imagine how weary the travellers would have been, having climbed the Mynydd from the low-lying land to the east. At this well they would rest, quench their thirst, bathe their aching limbs and perhaps seek a blessing. As they rested high above Porth Neigwl they would be able to gaze out over the sea towards the holy island, knowing that their journey was almost at an end.

Long ago Ffynnon Aelrhiw was not only a Christian holy well it was also famous for its healing properties, for as Myrddin Fardd noted, 'Many sick pilgrims travelled to it to obtain Saint Aelrhiw's blessing, and to sample its virtues ...' A book of 1828 (Cathrall's *History of North Wales*), which refers to the well as Ffynnon Aelrhiw, states that its waters were supposed to be excellent for treating disorders of the skin, particularly a condition called 'Man Aeliw', also referred to as 'the mark or spot of Aeliw'. The well water here was also said to have been famous for treating anaemia, owing to its high iron content.

But who was Saint Aelrhiw? In his book of *Welsh Saints*, published in 1853, Rees refers to Aelrhiw as a saint of uncertain date. Browne Willis in his Survey of Bangor, published earlier in 1721, refers to the saint as Eelrhyw or Delwfyw. Both Rees and Browne Willis quote the saint's festival date as September 9th. In 1907, however, Baring-Gould and Fisher stated that no saint called Aelrhiw, Eelrhyw or Delwfyw was found among the genealogies of the Welsh saints. This has led to speculation that there never was a saint called Aelrhiw, and that the well was dedicated to Y Ddelw Fyw (*'the living image'*), which is in fact the Holy Rood (i.e. an effigy of Christ on the cross). According to several 16th and 17th century Welsh Calendars the festival of the Holy Rood is September 9th which both Rees and Browne Willis record as the festival date of the problematic Saint Aelrhiw or Saint Eelrhyw.

Rhiw – Ffynnon Saint or Ffynnon Bron Llwyd

Sometimes referred to as Ffynnon Bron Llwyd, Ffynnon Saint is located in a remote spot, 300 feet up on the north-eastern slopes of Bron Llwyd, hence the alternative name. To reach the well, go to the main cross roads in Rhiw and take the road, signposted 'Plas yn Rhiw'. Walk down the steep hill past the road which leads to the National Trust property until you reach the plaque commemorating the opening of the new section of road. Go through the gate onto the old road, passing Tre Heli farm on the left. When you come to the junction with the new road cross over and take the track, signposted Ty'n y Parc. Stay on this track, first passing Ty'n y Parc and then some forestry sheds. Eventually, amidst the pine trees the track turns sharp right and ascends a steep hill. At the top of the hill, you will see a stone wall facing you; at this point turn left up some stone steps. Keeping the wall on your right, pass through the wooden gate and you will see the well.

Ffynnon Bron Llwyd is surrounded by rubble-built walls about 0.61m thick and 1.22m high. The stone-walled pool is 2.7 metres square and there are 2 sets of steps at the eastern end of the north and south sides to allow the water to be accessed from both directions. It is not clear if those steps have been constructed or if they are natural boulders which just happen to be lying there.

The well itself is covered with weed and ferns but the water from the spring is still visible within the basin. The water flows down the slope into the pool, and the outflow of water exits at the lower end to join a stream which flows down the hillside through the pine forest.

As its name suggests, Ffynnon Saint was originally a holy well although the masonry work is almost certainly post-medieval. However, it is possible that this well site may have been used centuries ago by medieval pilgrims. It was said to be a healing well, especially effective for treating eye conditions. Myrddin Fardd stated that local women used to come to this well on the morning of Ascension Day so that they could bathe their eyes and throw pins into the water as a thanks offering. Today the well is in a fairly dilapidated condition, although it is completely natural and therefore worth the effort required to reach it. Since the site is situated within a forest on the lower slopes of Mynydd Rhiw, the remoteness of this location affords the visitor a welcome air of peace and tranquillity.

Rhiw – Ffynnon Pant

Ffynnon Pant, the Well in the Hollow, is in a rather poor condition but it still contains clean water. It is located in a field below the Abersoch to Aberdaron road but it is not easily accessed. The well, which has now been incorporated into a modern field wall, has a stone wall around it (about 1 metre from side to side) but it is open at the front. It is not known if this well had any religious or healing significance, but in times past it was certainly used as a source of domestic water by the inhabitants of the area. Therefore the enclosing wall was probably built by the local people to protect their water supply.

Ffynnon Pant seems to have been a very reliable water source, for as we shall see in due course, in times of drought when other wells in the district had dried up Ffynnon Pant was still flowing, and people sometimes had to walk considerable distances to it to collect water for their daily needs. Ffynnon Pant, like many others on the peninsula, was used as a water supply until the 20th century when, following the completion of the Cwm Ystradllyn public water scheme in the late 1950s, the whole peninsula was provided with piped water.

Rhiw – Ffynnon Rofyr

Ffynnon Rofyr is situated on the side of the hill at Mynydd Rhiw, below the communication mast which looks out towards Rhoshirwaen. This well, which is completely natural, is roughly circular and measures about one metre in diameter. The water is about 20cm. deep and, on leaving the well, it flows down the slope towards a cottage. Ffynnon Rofyr would have been the only source of domestic water for the inhabitants of that cottage prior to the completion of the Cwm Ystradllyn water scheme in 1959. There is no record of it having been a holy well.

Rhiw – Ffynnon Conion

Ffynnon Conion is situated due south of Mynydd Rhiw between the Mynydd and the village of Rhiw. Nearby are several dwellings, including Conion and Conion Uchaf. Clearly, at one time, Ffynnon Conion would have provided these houses and cottages with their water supply. The well is about 0.61m square and it has a lid which must be lifted by hand. Today the site has been abandoned, for it is now filled with stones, although the water continues to overflow, causing the surrounding ground to be wet and marshy.

A 1930s diary written by Griffith Thomas of Ael y Bryn, Rhiw (extracts from which can be found on the excellent Rhiw.com website) provides us with some interesting information about the wells in the Rhiw area, including this one. Dated Friday 8th September 1933, an entry records that the water at Ffynnon Conion had dried up owing to the exceptionally dry weather. On Monday 11th he writes that water was being carried from Ffynnon Pant each day. On Saturday 16th the writer observes that the whole of the past week has been exceptionally dry and that there was still no sign of rain. He bemoans the fact that all the local wells were drying up, and that people were still being forced to walk to Ffynnon Pant to collect water. These diary entries illustrate, not only the inconvenience of having to fetch water each day from a nearby spring, but also the unreliability of natural water supplies during extended periods of drought. In Llŷn many people living in isolated houses and small communities depended upon natural wells and springs for their water supplies right up until the middle of the 20th century.

A short distance to the south-east of Conion is the site of an Iron Age stone fort, and and therefore it is possible that there may have been a connection long ago between Ffynnon Conion and that prehistoric site.

Uwchmynydd – Ffynnon Fair or Saint Mary's Well

Ffynnon Fair is a natural spring near the foot of the cliff on Mynydd Mawr. Above the cliff is the site of a small chapel called Tŷ Fair, the last of a series of chapels along the pilgrim route. Here the pilgrims would not only give thanks for the journey completed thus far but, gazing out at Ynys Enlli before them, they would also offer a prayer for a safe crossing of the dangerous Sound with its fast currents and whirlpools. It is said that mariners and fishermen also prayed at this chapel in the hope of securing a safe voyage.

Tŷ Fair was closely associated with Saint Mary's well at the foot of the cliff. Having scrambled down the cliff path pilgrims would take a drink from Saint Mary's well, which is close to Saint Mary's cave. This well is famed throughout Llŷn and beyond, partly on account of its associations with pilgrims and legends, partly because of the purity of its water and partly because it looks directly across the sound towards the holy island.

After modern day visitors have driven across the cattle grid at the end of the road which leads to Mynydd Mawr they will be able to park on the grassy National Trust land immediately beyond. Ffynnon Fair can be reached by walking back across the cattle grid and then taking the path across a slightly upward-sloping, grassy area with Mynydd Mawr to the right and Mynydd Gwyddel to the left. Proceed along this path to the edge of the cliff, where you will find a set of hazardous stone steps (known as Grisiau Mair – *grisiau*: staircase) cut into the cliff face.

Great care is required when descending these steps (for they can be extremely dangerous, especially in wet weather). Considerable care is also required when scrambling over the rocks below. In 1904 a 16 year old girl tragically lost her life, on these rocks when she was part of a party who were enjoying a family picnic near Ffynnon Fair. A newpaper report of the incident records that the girl was standing on the rocks very near to the edge of the sea when an unusually large wave rushed in and carried her away. Eventually men with ropes arrived on the scene but nothing more was seen of the girl. Several days later her body was recovered, and it was buried in Aberdaron churchyard where her gravestone reads, 'In loving memory of Joan Abbot Parry, daughter of Judge Parry of Manchester, born September 19th 1888 drowned near Saint Mary's Well September 6th 1904.'

Having reached the rocks, people searching for the well must clamber across them to the right but the well is not easy to find. Ffynnon Fair, which lies in a natural, grass-lined triangular rock basin, is situated above the shore line and is filled by a trickle of water which descends the rockface into the basin. The remarkable thing is that this spring disappears completely beneath the sea water at very high tide, but when the tide has ebbed again the water in the basin is totally pure and free from the taste of salt. This well has the appearance of yet another ordinary rock pool but a taste test of the water will confirm whether or not Ffynnon Fair has been found.

An old legend states that, if ancient pilgrims could take a mouthful of water from this well and run up the stone steps to the top of the cliff without swallowing any of it, they would be blessed and assured of a safe crossing. There are slight variations to this story, one being that, having reached the cliff top, the traveller had to run three times around the small chapel without swallowing or spilling any of the water.

Ieuan Lleyn, in his *Journey through Lleyn*, mentioned this well 'and many other Papal relics such as the hooves of Mary's horse and the likes.' There are several traditional stories of the Virgin Mary visiting this place. Near Ffynnon Fair the sea has carved from the rock a hollow which is shaped like a horse's hoof and, according to local legend, this is the hoof mark left by the Virgin Mary's horse as it galloped away. Nearby there is another mark in the rock which looks like the imprint of a hand. Local legend would have us believe that this is the imprint of the Virgin Mary's hand as she leaned forward to take a drink from the well. Such tales about the visit of the Virgin Mary to the area were dismissed as 'relics of Popery' by Ieuan Lleyn, for he was an ardent Protestant. His mother's father, Siarl Marc, was a prominent 18th century Calvinistic Methodist chapel leader and preacher.

R. S. Thomas, a former vicar of Aberdaron and a renowned Welsh poet, has immortalised Saint Mary's well in his poem 'Ffynnon Fair'.

Uwchmynydd – Ffynnon Tŷ Mawr

The AONB team reported that this well was overgrown although clear water could be seen beneath the vegetation. The author has not attempted to locate this well although a property on the right hand side of the road before you reach the cattle grid near the grass-covered National Trust car park is called Tŷ Mawr. Therefore Ffynnon Tŷ Mawr may be near this property. In days gone by it was probably used as a domestic water supply. Nothing more is known about the well's history.

Uwchmynydd – Ffynnon Armon

This well is named after Saint Garmon, and according to Francis Jones there are 10 Welsh wells which bear this saint's name. Garmon Sant is the Welsh name for Saint Germanus, Bishop of Auxerre in France who, it is said, was sent by the Pope to Britain, accompanied by Lupus, the Bishop of Troyes, shortly after the Romans had left. The purpose of this visit was to impart orthodox Roman teaching to the followers of the Celtic Church. According to Nennius, Germanus came again in about 447. It is believed that, when he returned he spent time in the Celtic parts of Britain; it is certainly true that his name is commemorated in place names in both North Wales (Betws Garmon and Llanarmon) and Cornwall (Saint Germans).

Many of the early saints, who were from the families of tribal leaders, had military knowledge and they were not averse to gathering an army together so that they could defeat hostile tribespeople who were threatening their way of life. In his *Life of Saint Germanus* the cleric Constantius of Lyon, who was a contemporary of the saint and a friend of Bishop Lupus,

185

recounts an incident in which Germanus led a small band of Britons to victory against a much larger force of Picts and Saxons without a blow being struck. Germanus devised a plan whereby he ordered his men to advance through a narrow valley shouting 'Alleluia' at the tops of their voices before they came in sight of the enemy. Unable to see the approaching force, the enemy soldiers were convinced that they were about to face a vastly superior army and so they fled in disorder. According to the story many were drowned as they tried to escape across a river. Tradition leads us to believe that the site of this battle was at Mold in Flintshire where there is still a place called Maes Garmon.

When the AONB team visited Ffynnon Armon it was overgrown and its brick wall had collapsed. The author is not aware of its precise location and therefore he has not visited this well. Nothing is known about its history. However, since Saint Garmon's cult was fairly strong in North Wales, it is probable that, in times past, Ffynnon Armon was looked upon as a holy well. It probably also served as a fresh water supply as was the case with many of the springs on the peninsula.

Uwchmynydd – Ffynnon Cernydd

When visited by the AONB team Ffynnon Cernydd was overgrown and the water was neither clean nor clear. This well on the lower slopes of Mynydd Mawr is identified by name on the O S Explorer map No. 253, to the north of Safn Pant Farm. It is enclosed on three sides but is open on the eastern side. At one time it almost certainly provided water for the nearby farm but nothing further is known about its history which remains shrouded in mystery.

Uwchmynydd – Ffynnon Safn Pant

In 2005 the AONB team reported that this well required cleaning and that a new lid was needed. It is situated behind the farmhouse at Safn Pant Farm on Mynydd Mawr. For many years it obviously provided water for the farm. It is not known if it was reputed to have any special powers.

The Wells of Ynys Enlli (Bardsey)

Tomos Jones, who was an 11 year old boy in 1891, lived on a small Enlli farm called Tŷ Newydd. He recalls in the book *Tomos the Islandman* that, although there are no rivers on the island, there are plenty of natural wells. A legend states that, in the distant past, a giant leapt from a small offshore island called Maen Bugel onto Ynys Enlli and when he landed his feet sank into the ground thus creating the wells. It is known from the archaeology discovered on Enlli that the island was inhabited from the Neolithic times onwards. Clearly it was these natural springs which provided essential supplies of fresh water for the island's inhabitants, although at least one of them, and probably one or two others, also became renowned for healing properties. It is surprising that none of the named wells on this sacred island is dedicated to a saint – unless, of course some of the original names have been lost over time. There is very little documantary historical evidence about the wells of Ynys Enlli. RCAHMW mentions Ffynnon Corn but Francis Jones in his book on the Holy Wells of Wales does not mention any of the wells on the island.

The most important of the Enlli wells are:

Ffynnon Corn

Ffynnon Corn, which is a Grade II listed monument, is one of the main wells on the island and, since it nestles at the base of Mynydd Enlli fairly close to the remains of the old abbey, it was probably this well which provided the monks with a supply of fresh water. It is described as the island's most reliable water source.

Ffynnon Corn is to be found on the northern side of the island behind the chapel, above the site of the old abbey and fairly close to the path which leads up the mountain. Tomos Jones stated that it was situated beneath a rock with a wall built around it. He also said that the water here was pure and cold and that it never dried up. He was under the impression that the monks on the island had excavated it and constructed the retaining wall. This well was almost certainly the main water source for the monks and it is still used as a source of water for people on the island today.

A well described by the RCAHMW in considerable detail but unnamed, may be Ffynnon Corn. The entry reads 'It is built into a cleft at the foot of a rock outcrop and consists of a stone basin 2ft 3ins by 3ft 6ins. The surviving masonry is very well-built and includes some thin slabs of yellow gritstone. There is a step or shelf at the back beneath which is a large slab containing the rounded inlet. This step and the side ledges are now covered by water, which may be at a higher level than originally. A considerable quantity of fallen stone suggests that there was a superstructure of some kind, and although there are now no datable features, its character and the fact that this is the island's most reliable source of water, point to the masonry being early, probably medieval.'

The surviving masonry lies entirely below ground level but the outcrop of rock beneath which it lies is clearly visible. The early structure below the water level is built of stone but just below ground level there is some much later brickwork. Today the well is accessed by means of a hinged cover and the well-site is protected by a wooden gate. When first viewed and photographed in 2012 the cover was a wooden one which was covered in roofing felt. When visited again in 2015 the previous cover had been replaced by a more modern one, made of green plastic.

Ffynnon Owen Rolant or Ffynnon Uchaf

A little higher than Ffynnon Corn is another well called Ffynnon Owen Rolant or Ffynnon Uchaf. According to Tomos Jones the water in this well was not as pure as that in Ffynnon Corn. He also mentioned that, during the very hot Enlli summers, its waters frequently dried up. Its precise location is not known although the name would suggest that it was situated on the higher ground, further up Mynydd Enlli. It was supposed to have possessed some curative powers and was ideal for bathing sore feet and legs.

Ffynnon Barfau

In a rock higher up the mountainside are two natural basins which fill with fresh water. Tomos the Islandman likened them to two skulls, presumably inverted. According to legend these two basins were formed when a giant placed his feet on this rock and leapt from it onto another rock, Maen Bugail, which is in the middle of Bardsey Sound. Tradition also states that this well is called Ffynnon Barfau (*barfau*: beards) because this was the place where the monks of Enlli shaved or trimmed their beards. This was the explanation told to Tomos Jones by his grandfather. According to Tomos, the monks were able to shave here because they could see their reflections clearly in the deep, clear water. He also stated that above the well there are two holes in the rock and he was told that these little compartments were where the monks once stored their beard-trimming implements. According to Myrddin Fardd the two basins, one measuring '20 ins long by 9 ins wide and 2 feet deep and the other is 20ins long by 7ins wide and 2 feet deep', are always full of water in both summer and winter.

Ffynnon Dalar or Ffynnon Bryn Baglau

On the slope of Bryn Baglau, on the northern side of the road leading from the monastery to the landing creek at Y Cafn, is Ffynnon Dalar, also sometimes referred to as Ffynnon Baglau. Situated a short distance from Ffynnon Corn, according to tradition it was considered to be a very effective healing well for the pilgrims, capable of treating many complaints. It is alleged that its healing properties were so remarkable that, after visiting this well, many disabled pilgrims were completely cured and were able to abandon their sticks and crutches, which they left on the nearby Bryn Baglau (*bryn*: hill; *baglau*: crutches). The pilgrims, having walked many miles to reach the island, would also wash their aching feet and legs in the water at Ffynnon Dalar to soothe them. Elfed Gruffydd states that, according to local folklore, fairies and elves gathered at Ffynnon Dalar every year to hold their revelries. (E. Gruffydd: *Llŷn*)

Ffynnon Dolysgwydd

This spring is located on reasonably level ground in a field at the southern end of the main part of the island near the landing creek, Y Cafn. It lies beside an area of exposed rock to the west of Pen Cristin. The spring has been enclosed within a very low brick wall to create a reasonably large pool. According to legend, miracles were performed at this well, although it is not known whether they were miracles of healing or of some other kind.

Ffynnon Weirglodd Bach

This well is situated in Cae Ffynnon, south west of Tŷ Pellaf and south-east of the road which runs to Y Cafn, the landing point for the island. Some sources state that it had a reputation as a holy well, although nothing further is known about its history. Nothing remains of the well now apart from some stones in a hollow in the ground.

Ffynnon Dyno Goch

Situated in a field to the south of Dyno Goch and beneath a clawdd bank with a post and wire fence above it, Ffynnon Dyno Goch has stone walls below ground level and cover on top to protect it. The Bardsey Island Trust leaflet states that, once upon a time, a guardian eel was believed to have lived in it.

Other Wells on Enlli

In days gone by the occupants of every farm and house on Enlli would have needed a supply of water for their daily needs and these would have been met by the numerous springs and wells on the island. Here are some of the other named Enlli wells: Ffynnon Cae Dŵr, Ffynnon Carreg, Ffynnon Defaid, Ffynnon Ddiarana, Ffynnon Waen Cristin, Ffynnon Defaid and Ffynnon Tan 'Radell.

H. D. Williams in his book, *Ynys Enlli*, states that there are no springs in the part of the island near the lighthouse, although a couple of springs have beern discovered in the southern part of the island. Williams says that, in the past, when the lighthouse was manned, those living there throughout the year would store rainwater in large underground tanks. During periods of drought, when the tanks were dry and there was no fresh water emerging from the springs on the island, the lighthouse ship would come all the way from Holyhead, carrying supplies of fresh water.

He also states that throughout the year, in days gone by, many houses on Enlli would store as much water as they could in barrels so that, if ever the wells dried up during periods of drought, they would have sufficient water for themselves and for their livestock. This illustrates the difficulties people often faced in remote areas when the natural wells and springs dried up owing to a lack of rainfall.

Bibliography and Sources

Anderson, M.D. *Looking for History in British Churches* Murray 1957

AONB *A Study into the Condition of Wells within the Pen Llŷn Area of Outstanding Natural Beauty 2005*.

Archaeologia Cambrensis – various volumes

Bardsey Island Trust – a leaflet entitled 'Wells on Bardsey'.

Baring-Gould, S. & Fisher, J. *The Lives of the Saints*, Four Volumes, Honourable Society of Cymmrodorion, London 1907.

Bassett, T.M. & Davies, B.L. (Editors) *Atlas of Caernarfonshire* Gwynedd Rural Council 1977

Bond, Roland, *Nefyn: the Story of and Ancient Gwynedd Town and Parish* Gwasg Carreg Gwalch 2008

Bord, Janet, an article entitled *Cursing not Curing: The darker Side of Holy Wells*

Bowen, E.G. *The Saints of Gwynedd* TCHS Vol 9 (1948)

Browne-Willis, *Survey of Bangor* London 1721

Burris, N. & Stiff, J. *Walks on the Llŷn Peninsula Part I* Gwasg Carreg Gwalch 1995

Dodd, A.H. *A Short History of Wales: Welsh Life and Customs from Prehistoric Times to the Present Day* Batsford Ltd London 1972

Dyfed Archaeological Trust, *Medieval and Post-Medieaval Holy Wells Project 2011*

Edwards, Nancy, An article entitled *Holy Wells and Early Christian Archaeology*

Eifion, Alltud, *Ffynhonnau'r Gest yn Eifionydd* in Llygad y Ffynnon (Cylchlythyr Cymdeithas Ffynhonnau Cymru Rhif 19 Nadolig 2005

Fardd, Myrddin, *Llên Gwerin Sir Gaernarfon*, Caernarfon 1908

Fardd, Myrddin, *'Gleanings from God's Acre'* 1903

Fenton, R., *Tours in Wales* (1804-13) a supplement to *Archaeolgia Cambrensis* 1917

Gerald of Wales *Journey Through Wales and The Description of Wales* Penguin Classics 2004 Edition

Gleasure, Eira and James, *Criccieth : A Heritage Walk*, Cymdeithas Hanes Eifionydd, Wales, 2003.

Green, Miranda, An article entitled *The Religious Symbolism of Llyn Cerrig Bach and Other Early Sacred Water Sites*

Gruffydd, E *Llŷn* (adapted from the Welsh by Gwyneth Owen) Gwasg Carreg Gwalch 2003

Harlech, Lord *Illustrated Regional Guides to Ancient Monuments Vol. 5* HMSO 1948

Harrison, Ted An article entitled *Holy Waters* 2011

Heath, J. *Ancient Echoes: the early history of a Welsh peninsula* Gwasg Carreg Gwalch 2006

Hodgman, C. & Dyas, D. *Pilgrimage* – an article in the BBC History Magazine June 2013.

Hilling, J.B. *The Historic Architecture of Wales* University of Wales Press (1976)

Hughes, D.G. Lloyd, *Pwllheli, an Old Welsh Town and its History* Gwasg Gomer 1991

Hughes H. & North H.L. *The Old Churches of Snowdonia* republished by Snowdonia National Park Society 1984

Huws, Howard (Chairman of Cymdeithas Ffnhonnau Cymru) An article entitled *The Holy Wells of Wales*. 2012

Hyde-Hall, Edmund *A Description of Caernarvonshire 1809-11*

Johns, C.N. *The Celtic Monasteries of North Wales* in TCHS Vol. 21 1960

Jones, E.G. *A Survey of the Ancient and Present State of the County of Caernarvon by William Williams of Llandegai Cantref Lleyn*, TCHS Vol. 39 1978

Jones, Francis *The Holy Wells of Wales* University of Wales Press 1954

Jones, Jennie *Tomos the Islandman* Gwasg Carreg Gwalch 1964

Jones, R. Gerallt *A Place in the Mind: A Boyhood in Llŷn* Gomer 2004

Leland, *Itinerary in England and Wales 1536-9* Ed. Lucy Toulmin Smith 1964

Lleyn, Ieuan 'A Journey through Lleyn' 1799 – a letter written by Ieuan Lleyn to a friend in 1799 and reproduced on the Rhiw.com website.

Lynch, Frances *Gwynedd* HMSO London 1995

Miller, Molly *The Saints of Gwynedd: Studies in Celtic History* Boydell Press 1979

Morris, *Portmadoc and its Resources* 1856

National Dictionary of Wales

Newspapers – various titles and dates

Ordnance Survey Maps – Explorer Series (2.5 inches to 1 mile) Nos. 253 and 254.

Parry, H. Typscript copy of *The History of Nefyn and District* CRO XM/2002/198

Peate, Iorwerth *The Welsh House* Llanerch Press 2004 but first published 1940

Pennant, Thomas *Tours in Wales 1773-6 Vol.III*

Phillips, Charles, *Kings and Queens of Britain* Hermes House, undated

Rattue, James, *The Living Stream* Boydell and Brewer 1995

Rees, Elizabeth, *Celtic Saints and their Landscape* History Press 2001

Rees, W.J. *Lives of the Cambro-British Saints* Llandovery 1853

Rhiw.com website

Rhŷs, Sir John. *Celtic Folklore*, Chapter 6 entitled *The Folklore of the Wells* Oxford 1901

Robb, G. *The Genius of the Celts* BBC History Magazine Christmas 2013

Robbins, N.S. A paper entitled '*A regional hydrogeological assessment of Wales*'

Royal Commission of Ancient and Historic Monuments in Wales: Caernarfonshire Vols. II (Central) and III (West)

Russell, Miles, *King Arthur's Legend* an article published in the BBC History Magazine, Feb. 2016.

Shepherd, Val, An article entitled *Wells and Trees.*

Swann, June, an article entitled *Shoes Concealed in Buildings* 1996

Touchstone for Cadw, an online study entitled *Celtic Saints, Spiritual Places and Pilgrimage.*

Transactions of the Caernarfonshire Historical Society – various volumes

Tithe Maps of the Llŷn Peninsula -various

Williams, David *The Dating old Welsh Houses Project: Bodwrdda* June 2012

Williams, Glanmor, *The Reformation in Caernarfonshire* TCHS Vol. 27 1966

Williams, H.D. *Ynys Enlli* Gwasg ar y Graig 1979

Further enjoyable reading on History and Heritage

Visit our website for further information:
www.carreg-gwalch.com

Orders can be placed on our
On-line Shop

More Books
about Llŷn

Visit our website for further information:
www.carreg-gwalch.com

Orders can be placed on our
On-line Shop